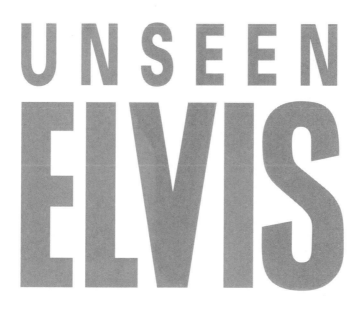

UNSEEN ELVIS

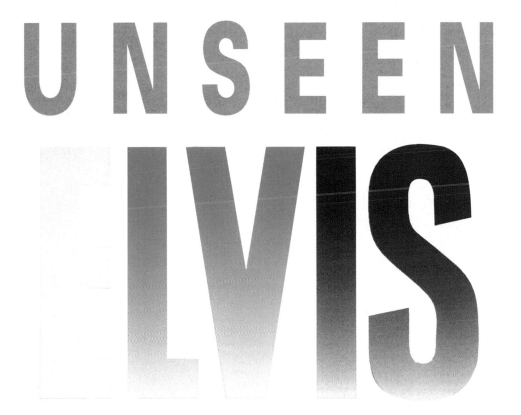

UNSEEN ELVIS

Candids of the King

From the Collection of Jim Curtin

A Bulfinch Press Book
Little, Brown and Company
Boston   Toronto   London

Text copyright © 1992 by G&H Soho, Ltd.
Captions copyright © 1992 by Jim Curtin
Illustrations from the collection of Jim Curtin

First Edition

Library of Congress Cataloging-in-Publication Data

Curtin, Jim.
     Unseen Elvis: candids of the king from the collection of Jim Curtin.—1st ed.
    p. cm.
  "A Bulfinch Press book."
  ISBN 0-8212-1912-X
  1. Presley, Elvis, 1935–1977—Portraits. 2. Rock musicians—United States—
Portraits. I. Title.
ML88.P76C87 1992
782.42166'092—dc20
[B]   91-30712

Bulfinch Press is an imprint and trademark of Little, Brown and Company (Inc.)
Published simultaneously in Canada by Little, Brown & Company (Canada) Limited

PRINTED IN THE UNITED STATES OF AMERICA

In memory of my parents

My mother, Louise M. Curtin (1921–1991), who stood by and supported me,
and who also tolerated my outrageous hobby—Elvis

My father, James J. Curtin, Jr. (1925–1988), who first turned me on to Elvis
(with the *Ed Sullivan Show*) and bought me my first
Elvis record (a 45 of "Return to Sender")

CONTENTS

Elvis has been an important part of my life since the first time I saw him. It was 1956, and he was performing on the Ed Sullivan show. His style just captivated me—the movements, look, voice, mannerisms, talent. This guy's wild, I thought. I was seven years old, and I was hooked forever.

So was America. We grew up with him, and so did our cameras. We started snapping him with our Brownies in the '50s, went on to give him Instamatic red eyes in the '60s, pointed and shot in the '70s. If Elvis had lived into the '80s and '90s, he would have become America's favorite home video.

Don't judge the photographs in this book on technical considerations. They're not professional—they're family pictures, clumsily captured records of important events. The people who shot them were overcome by emotion. This was the moment they'd long dreamed of: they were meeting Elvis.

I'm sure most of the unknown photographers represented here lovingly tucked their snapshots into picture albums next to all the other people they cherished. "The trip to Graceland" probably shared space with "Christmas '58" and "Graduation Day."

Look how young everybody is in the photos shown in the first chapter. Elvis' first fans were teenagers—girls, mostly. He shook 'em up with the way he moved on stage. Girls came to Memphis from all over, and waited outside the gates for a glimpse of Elvis. Look at the proud expressions on their faces. They got Elvis to pose with them! To smile just for them! They'll be able to show everybody they know!

And Elvis loved his fans. He knew his success depended on them, and he never took them for granted.

Once he got out of the Army, he'd grown up somewhat, and so had his audience. "It's Now or Never" was played on stations that catered to the parents of the kids who swooned to "Heartbreak Hotel." They became fans, too.

I didn't have much money growing up; summers would go by without an ice cream cone. I did a lot of odd jobs even as a young boy—returning used soda bottles for the refund, shoveling snow, painting addresses on houses, shining shoes. I'd hit every bar as far as 52nd and Market in Philadelphia shining shoes for a quarter, and practically every place I went into had Elvis Presley playing on the jukebox.

In 1962, my dad bought me my first record player for $38. Of course, I bought an Elvis record, "Return to Sender," to play on it. Then I bought my first album, "Elvis' Golden Records Volume I." The more I looked at the picture of him on the cover, the more intrigued I was. I decided I wanted every one of his records.

That's how I became a collector. I called every record shop in the Delaware Valley, all 116 of them, and drove to each one. By 1966, I owned every LP, album, and 45 Elvis had recorded.

Then I got in deeper. I wanted every 78. I wanted his foreign releases. When I got involved with the foreign fan clubs, I discovered that every foreign country had different covers. From 1966 to 1971, I went international. I was intrigued by any little differences in the releases—the cover art, the lyrics. I accumulated 5,000 records—652 songs — from 57 different countries.

My dad first turned me on to Elvis on screen. He took me see *King Creole.* Then I went back and saw it six times in one day. My favorite movie, though, is *Jailhouse Rock,* which I've seen about 50 times. I have every one of Elvis' films on both 16 millimeter and video.

Still, it wasn't until 1971 that I got to see Elvis in person for the first time. I paid $50 for a fifteenth row seat on the floor that sold for $15 at the Philadelphia Spectrum. From seeing the documentary *Elvis: That's The Way It Is,* I had a basic idea of the jumpsuits he wore and how he began a concert. But actually being there was different. When the lights went down and "2001: A Space Odyssey" came up, I got a supernatural feeling. I'd idolized this man since

I was a little boy, and here he was in front of me.

After that, my passion to collect Elvis material took off. I didn't just want records but photos (I now have 25,000 of them, organized chronologically) and everything else Elvis related. That was a tall order; Elvis Presley Enterprise Products began manufacturing in 1956 and cranked out a lot of different products—menus, tour books of Graceland, buttons, lipstick, wallets, toy guitars, handkerchiefs, you name it. Things slowed down when he went into the Army in 1958, then built up again in the early '60s. The new products still came with a 1956 copyright.

Starting to collect this stuff more than a decade later put me far behind the game, which was frustrating and expensive. Elvis lipstick was a dollar in 1956. Today, if you can find one on the original card, you'll pay $1,000. Still, I managed to develop a collection which has made me an Elvis authority and a resource for numerous projects, including the best-selling Elvis poster in history and eight calendars.

I had several face-to-face encounters with Elvis. After seeing *Elvis: Aloha from Hawaii* in 1973, I decided I had to meet him. But how? Millionaires have tried to bribe their way into Graceland without success. I knew I'd need something different. The closest thing to Elvis is his music, so I designed a custom guitar and commissioned the Gibson Corporation to build it—a black acoustic instrument with Elvis' name on the finger board and two crowns inlaid in mother of pearl. With the case it cost $2,000 and took almost a year to make. Gibson shipped it to me in June 1974, a few days late to try to get it to him during his Philadelphia tour.

So I set my sights on Las Vegas, three months away. At the time, I was working at a supermarket in South Philadelphia, making $122 a week. I saved every nickel for a year to put together the money for my scheme to meet Elvis. When I flew to Vegas, I was afraid to put the guitar in luggage, so I bought another seat for the guitar.

Once I got out there, I managed to meet

Vernon Presley at the Hilton, by the dollar one-armed bandits. I explained that I had this $2,000 guitar that I wanted to give to Elvis. He said, "I'll see what I can do." I saw 29 shows in Las Vegas, paying $150 per show to sit right up front so I could shake his hand. It was worth it, though. I got 32 handshakes.

A lot of people used to take my picture, too, in Vegas, because I'd started dressing like Elvis. I think he got a kick out of it; he'd come right over to me on stage during his show.

Still, after a few days with no word from Vernon, I almost gave up. Then one night, I was watching the show and Vernon found me and said, "Elvis wants to meet you. Go back to your suite and I'll call you. Then you can come up to see Elvis." At 5:00 A.M., he finally did, and I asked him over the phone if I could take a picture of Elvis, and he said no. Then he softened a little and said to bring my camera, but he couldn't promise anything. At 5:10 I went upstairs, past the guards on the 30th floor and into Elvis' suite.

Charlie Hodge offered me a Coke and said, "Hand me the guitar, I'll put it in tune." Soon

Elvis walked in, dressed in black, sunglasses on. He smiled at me and walked past, through a beaded curtain. After a while, Vernon waved me in through that curtain, and I entered Elvis' living quarters. Everything was white and gold French Provincial, and there was a portrait of Elvis in his Army uniform with his parents hanging over the couch. I sat on the couch with his girlfriend, Sheila Ryan. Elvis walked out and said hello. I said, "Elvis, I've waited all my life to meet you." He gave me that little smile, then introduced me to Sheila Ryan, and sat on the couch with his arm around her. He was super-polite, and very down to earth.

I got the guitar, and leaned it in its case, upright against the coffee table in front of Elvis and sat down next to Elvis. I made sure my knee touched his, I couldn't believe that Elvis was sitting right next to me. Without touching the guitar, Elvis tilted his head and read the inscription on the fingerboard, then he asked me why did I put the crowns on the guitar. I said that I saw his movie *That's the Way It Is* and that he had a tan guitar with stars on it. I told him that I thought he was bigger than a star, that he was the King. Then he stood up and said, "Come here, you," and gave me a big hug. He picked up my guitar, put his leg up on the coffee table, and played and sang "Baby, What Do You Want Me to Do?"

Here I am holding the guitar I had made for Elvis.

After Elvis hugged me, I asked him if I could take a couple of pictures, and he said okay. Joe Esposito shot them, but the pictures didn't come out. I called Vernon at his office, and he said he'd try to help me if I came back to Las Vegas again. I got there in March 1975 with another $2,000 in gifts—a hand made leather karate belt with tigers carved into it, a 14K gold and turquoise ring shaped like a king's crown, and

18 hardback books on karate and other martial arts. Then I found out that Vernon had had a heart attack. I told my story to Joe Esposito, but I could tell he didn't believe me about my pictures not coming out and thought I just wanted to meet Elvis again. He said he couldn't promise anything, that Elvis had gained a lot of weight and wouldn't want any pictures.

Joe did call me to come to Elvis' dressing room. As soon as I walked in, Elvis said to Diane Goodman, his new girlfriend, "This is the fellow who gave me a beautiful guitar the last time I was here." After I gave Elvis the gifts I asked him, "Elvis, could I take a picture with you?" He lowered his head and wouldn't say a word. Joe jumped in: "Didn't I tell you not to ask him for pictures?" I said, "I know you hear a million stories, but the pictures I took didn't come out. I thought I'd ask the man personally."

It was Elvis who broke the tension. He promised me if I came to Memphis he would take the photos with the guitar again, because the guitar was in his home in Memphis. I then asked Elvis for a memento, something to bring back to Philadelphia to show a million people. He went into his dressing room and brought out one of his jumpsuits and handed it to me. Redd Foxx was there, and he said, "Now hug each other," and we did. I said, "I love you, Elvis," and he said, "I love you too."

That was the year I started impersonating Elvis. Fans seemed to like what I was doing. Then a friend of my mother's got me an audition at a hotel in Philadelphia. I got a band and an agent and on May 28, 1977—the same night Elvis was appearing at the Philadelphia Spectrum—I performed in public for the first time, at a Philadelphia club. Our next gig was the Great Gorge Playboy Club; then it was somewhere new every week, all around New Jersey, Pennsylvania, Maryland, Delaware, and New York. Finally, after 400 shows, I cut back.

I have spiritual feelings for Elvis, a closeness that I can't explain. That's why I do what I do. Something's making me do it. You know, my mother's due date for my birth was January 8, 1949, the same day as Elvis' birthday, but I was born six weeks earlier.

By the end, Elvis was a legend. He'd achieved more than any other entertainer in the world, and he rested on that. After 24 years of entertaining, including 1,100 concerts, he was burned out. His life just kind of crumbled: Recordings were slowing down, and the choice of material wasn't as good as in the old days. He and his wife had split up, he was estranged from the Colonel, and he'd lost a lot of his best friends. He was overweight and had a lot of health problems, and all his medications were taking their toll.

I'm proud of the photos on the following pages, and happy to share them with other Elvis fans. Cynics may wonder if the world really needs another book about Elvis, but unlike so many others, this book was created with love. It's a communal family photo album from his fans.

Any photo of Elvis that hasn't been published before is worth its weight in gold. It's like bringing him back to life for a split second. These photos tell the human side of Elvis, not just the superstar but the down-to-earth, regular guy, willing to give of himself to his friends and fans. Elvis gave away cars, houses, jewelry. He supported over 50 charities. He gave away millions of dollars. From 1961 to 1971, Elvis was the biggest single taxpayer in the U.S.—the I.R.S would come in and he'd say, "What do I owe you?" and write them a check.

The day after Elvis died, every store in the country ran out of his records. "Suspicious Minds," which was recorded in 1969, still sells one million copies a year. Over 700,000 people visit Graceland annually—the only residence that draws more is the White House.

Elvis' fans miss him, and even a lot of people who once put him down now realize he was a great person. He was a spiritual man, a generous man, a family man. He was someone I really admired, and I'll always be his fan. Elvis, we love you.

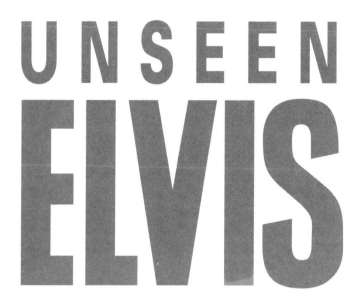

UNSEEN ELVIS

THE

FIFTIES

He broke upon the world like your mother's worst fears, strutting on stage with long hair and black leather, singing songs from the wrong side of town. If the squeaky-clean '50s was the nation's most conforming decade of the century, Elvis was its flip side. Wearing enough grease in his dirty blond hair to turn it black, Elvis made love to his microphone and rasped a hybrid of southern gospel, rhythm and blues, and that new beat soon to be known as rock 'n roll. He was just expressing himself, but his idiom would be adopted by a generation.

Elvis was an original, who came in the nick of time to rescue a generation stifling in suburban complacency. As Sun Records' owner Sam Phillips said, "I knew if I could find a white man who had the Negro sound and the Negro feel, I could make a billion dollars." The throne was ready; the ticket was bought for the ride to the top of the charts. To his fans, even Elvis' death wouldn't interrupt his reign.

His beginnings were humble. The Presleys—Vernon, Gladys, and Elvis—were a poor family struggling to make ends meet in early-'50s Memphis, where they'd moved from Mississippi. They lived in public housing for a few years until Gladys' $4 a day nurse's aide job pushed them over the eligibility ceiling. When the Memphis Housing Authority evicted them, the Presleys moved from their small but well-maintained apartment in the public Lauderdale Courts to a dingy, $52 a month apartment on downtown Cypress Street.

Music had a powerful hold on Elvis from childhood. Gladys bought him his first guitar for $12.95—ironically, it was something she did just to distract him from the $55 bicycle he'd really been asking for. He soon figured out how to pick out a few chords, pestering a couple of guitar-playing uncles for help. Living along the Mississippi, the young boy grew up with musical influences as rich as the soil. Every Sunday and Wednesday, Elvis joined his mother for revivals at the Pentecostal Assembly of God Church, where he learned to sing spirituals. As a teenager, one of his favorite forms of entertainment was to attend all-night sings, where he was spellbound by the full lineup of top gospel quartets and quintets. Gospel provided the lyrics, but the beat usually ranged from swing to soul. These shows transformed church events into fast-paced entertainment complete with patter, full bands, choreography, costumes, and fancy hairdos.

From the nearby black part of town, Elvis was exposed to the black gospel tradition that was slowly evolving into R&B, and he probably tuned in often to WDIA, the South's first black radio station and a key factor in popularizing the blues.

Elvis graduated from high school in 1953 and soon began contributing wages to the family's income, which allowed them to move again, this time to their own frame house on Alabama Street. It was in their old neighborhood, near Lauderdale Courts, where many of their friends stilled lived. It was pretty crowded inside, with Elvis on the couch, grandmother Minnie Mae on a cot in the dining room, and Vernon and Gladys in the house's only bedroom. Elvis worked the summer of 1953 at Precision Tools, making shells for the Army. His $66 weekly paycheck outstripped his father's, but monotony and hassles with the foreman over the length of his hair soon prompted Elvis to look for other work. At summer's end, he began a year's stint driving a truck and working in the warehouse at Crown Electric. Even though Elvis took a pay cut down to about $41 a week after taxes, he enjoyed the job more.

During this period, Elvis was considering a musical career as a gospel singer, although he hadn't taken any formal steps in that direction. Gospel was his lifelong favorite type of music. He'd befriended members of a popular Memphis gospel group, the Blackwoods, and hung around with their younger, feeder group called the Songfellows. Elvis joined both groups for

occasional rehearsals, and the Blackwoods sang backup for Elvis at all-night sings where, as James Blackwood observed, Elvis liked to sing with his eyes closed and hips moving. Elvis did occasionally sing solo on the secular stage, covering Dean Martin hits between big band sets at the Eagle's Nest, a motel and nightclub complex on the outskirts of Memphis. His dearest hope, though, was that one day he'd be asked to fill in an opening with either the Blackwoods or the Songfellows.

On June 30, 1954, the day after winning first place on "Arthur Godfrey's Talent Scouts" show, R.W. Blackwood was killed in a plane crash. When Cecil Blackwood left the Song-fellows to take R.W.'s place in the Blackwoods, the Songfellows invited Elvis to join them. But by then it was too late for him to take advantage of what would once have seemed a golden opportunity. Declining the Songfellows, Elvis told them, somewhat sadly, that he'd already signed a contract to sing the blues.

Actually, he was about to help invent a new kind of music—rock 'n roll. He would do it in the service of Memphis' Sun Records. How Sun found, signed, and promoted the young truck driver with a sexy sound is familiar to every Elvis fan and is the stuff of recording-industry legends. He stopped into the record-your-own-record sideline at Sun Studios and plunked down $2 to cut a record for Gladys' birthday gift. When office manager and former radio personality Marion Keisker heard him sing, she remembered her boss' perennial search for a white man with a black sound and rolled her own tape recorder. Sam Phillips wasn't too impressed by what he heard first time around, but sometime later Elvis went in and recorded "Without You" and "I'll Never Stand in Your Way." Marion tracked him down for an audition based on that recording.

Phillips introduced Elvis to musicians Scotty Moore, who also would sign on a few weeks later as Elvis' first manager, and Bill Black, and several difficult weeks of rehearsal began. The magic was still missing the night they came into Sun to record, so the boys took a break after a few hours' earnest practice and started cutting up in the studio, singing a "race" song with a funky beat. Phillips ran in and told them to do it again on tape.

"That's All Right (Mama)," released in 1954, had its first airplay on WHBQ, a white station that played songs by black bluesmen. The night it was scheduled to air, Elvis tuned in the station so his folks could hear it. Then, overcome with shyness and stage fright, he ducked out to the movies.

Gladys and Vernon walked the aisles to find him: The song had been received with so much enthusiasm deejay Dewey Phillips (no relation to Sam) was playing it over and over again and wanted to get Elvis into the studio for an interview.

Selling 20,000 copies, "That's All Right (Mama)" was a respectable regional hit for about six months. It earned Elvis a few hundred dollars, a few more local singing gigs, and a slot on two of the nation's most venerable country music shows, radio's "Grand Ole Opry" and television's "Louisiana Hayride."

Elvis' debut at the Opry on September 25, 1954 gave him a rude introduction to show business. With a few hours to fill before the show, Sam took the group into a nearby jukejoint to hear a piano player. Elvis went in briefly, seemed uncomfortable, then said he'd just wait outside. When Sam asked why, he told him, "My mama wouldn't want me in a place like this."

Showtime only made things worse. Jim Denny, the Opry's talent booker, accused Elvis of violating their deal by not bringing the entire band heard on the single—he couldn't believe Sam had produced such a big sound from just Elvis, Scotty, and Bill. Emcee Hank Snow was snide about Elvis' name, unnerving him just as he went on stage. Their reception was cool from the hidebound Opry audience. Finally, Denny snapped at Elvis as he was leaving, "We don't

play that kind of music around here. If I were you, I'd go back to driving a truck." Elvis cried all the way back to Memphis. Reporting to Crown Electric the next morning must have been a bitter disappointment.

Only three weeks after the Opry, "Louisiana Hayride" proved far more receptive to Elvis and the Blue Moon Boys, as Scotty and Bill were now called, offering them a year's contract. They took it—and spent weekends driving the 800 miles roundtrip from Memphis for a total of $42 each time for the band. On the plus side, they greatly expanded their audience over the airwaves and soon were completely wearing out Scotty's '54 Chevy Bel Air with steady tours throughout Louisiana, Arkansas, and Texas.

During this time, Scotty was Elvis' manager, collecting 10 percent of Elvis' share of any bookings he made. But Scotty preferred playing to booking, and all the road trips sleeping in the back of the car were wearing him down. He figured it would help to be able to concentrate on music instead of marketing. So after just six months, he handed the manager's hat over to Bob Neal, a Memphis deejay, and went back to being a full-time Blue Moon Boy. Bob drew up a simple contract that gave him 15 percent of the gross on any bookings he made, and the still-underage Elvis and his parents signed.

At first, it was Bob Neal's fame that drew people to the concerts he lined up in schoolhouses and advertised on his radio show and with fliers posted around town. His wife collected the cash—about $300 a night—in a cigar box. But soon enough it was Elvis who attracted the crowds. Word of his magnetism on stage plus the songs people were hearing on Bob Neal's radio program built a local following. The Blue Moon Boys played 200 gigs in 1955 alone.

Bob pushed the boys hard for strategic reasons as well as monetary ones. Beyond his own enthusiastic spinning, he was getting rebuffed in his radio-play promotional efforts. Elvis was rejected by country stations as too bluesy, by blues stations as too country, and Bob realized that it wasn't going to be the airwaves but personal appearances that would build his client's momentum.

His next managerial act was to change the terms of Scotty and Bill's membership in the Elvis juggernaut. They'd each been getting 25 percent and Elvis, 50 percent. But Elvis was the star, and Bob informed the boys that he was taking away their share and paying them a salary instead. Despite grumbles, they stayed.

Somehow, the boys also managed to pack in some Sun studio time among all the touring. Many consider these Sun recordings the height of Elvis' creative powers. He had a lot of fun, preferring long studio jam sessions to hours of rehearsal. His phrasing and delivery were inventive and playful; experimenting with songs by various artists, he would syncopate and jazz up the beat until the sound was his own. When he toured, Elvis the wild technician became Elvis the unfettered performer. The hip thrusts, splits, and amorous touch on the microphone were no affectations, no additions urged by his managers. Elvis was the Pelvis right from the start.

This sizzling new talent that was Elvis Presley caught Colonel Tom Parker's eye as early as 1954. Parker had heard about him from several of his talent scouts, and in February 1955 he helped Bob Neal book Elvis onto a two-week tour of Nevada. In May, he signed Elvis up with Hank Snow's southern tour. The Colonel must have gotten quite a jolt watching Elvis ignite a virtual riot in a crowd of 14,000 in Jacksonville, Florida, as he was recovering from a heart attack.

One month after being rejected in his audition for "Arthur Godfrey's Talent Scouts" television show, Elvis scored with an entire stadium. He was nearly smothered to death by a female crowd whipped to a feverish pitch by his performance and concluding whisper to the microphone, "Girls, I'll see you backstage." Several hundred took him at his word, and stadium security had to rescue him. Soon other artists on

Snow's circuit refused to perform in the slot following Elvis. He was too tough an act to follow.

Late in 1955, Colonel Parker started moving in on the position of Elvis' manager, laying the groundwork to take over from Bob Neal when his contract expired on March 15, 1956. One of his first acts was to get Elvis airplay north of the Mason-Dixon line, over radio station WERE in Cleveland, where deejay Bill Randle set the same clamor spinning as Dewey Phillips had in Memphis. Next, after long negotiations, he got RCA Records to purchase Elvis' contract from Sun Records for the then hefty price of $40,000 plus a bonus to cover future royalties Elvis would have received from Sun.

Sam Phillips probably regretted the deal for the rest of his life, but at the time he needed the cash, and Elvis was still purely a "live" phenomenon. His concerts were a lot more powerful than his record sales. Besides, Phillips' attention was elsewhere, focused on a new artist, Carl Perkins. Only with hindsight would Phillips see that he'd put his money on the wrong pair of blue suede shoes.

Just 21 years old, Elvis was jittery when he entered his first recording session for RCA on July 2, 1956. He paced the room as the musicians set up (his fine studio band included guitarist Chet Atkins), then sat down at the piano and unwound a little by crooning a few gospel tunes—a ritual with which Elvis would begin recording sessions for the rest of his life. Harmonizing behind him were members of the Jordanaires, a quartet from the "Grand Ole Opry," who would become Elvis' regular backup group.

Ray Charles' "I Got a Woman" was the first song recorded that day. During the first take, Elvis didn't just sing, he performed—moving around so much that the mike missed half of his vocals. Producer Steve Sholes ordered him to stand still. Meekly, Elvis complied, but during the second try the spark was missing. "Mr. Sholes, please don't make me stand still!" Elvis said. "If I can't move, I can't sing!" The magic returned with a solution that let Elvis shake it up: extra mikes suspended from the ceiling to catch the singer wherever he was. Elvis performed with passion, landing from a jump into a kneedrop that split the seam of his pants and whacking the guitar so hard his fingers bled.

He then recorded the song that would deepen his image by hitting the heart of any teenager who had ever lost in love. The eerie, despairing tone of "Heartbreak Hotel" came from the echo chamber in which it was recorded, the "ooohs" and "aaahs" of the Jordanaires, and Sholes' minimalist instrumentation. Combined, the elements provided the perfect backdrop for Elvis' bluesy, woebegone lament. With this 45, Elvis became the first artist to hit number one on all three *Billboard* charts—Hot 100, country, and rhythm and blues.

The day after the January release of "Heartbreak Hotel," Elvis, Scotty, and Bill made their first national television appearance on the Dorsey Brothers' "Stage Show." It would be the first of five performances, which sent "Heartbreak Hotel" up the charts with a bullet and landed Elvis appearances on the Milton Berle show, the Steve Allen show, and the Ed Sullivan show.

None of those shows gave fans the real Elvis. Steve Allen had him perform "Hound Dog" as part of a cutesy sketch with a live basset hound, while Sullivan dictated his musical selections and eventually, of course, shot his guest from the waist up—a phenomenon witnessed by an estimated 54 million Americans.

While the nation was won over, the critics were not. "Elvis," wrote Jack Gould of *The New York Times,* "might possibly be classified as an entertainer. Or, perhaps quite as easily, as an assignment for a sociologist." A week later, Gould elaborated. "When Presley executes his bumps and grinds," he wrote, "it must be remembered by the Columbia Broadcasting System that even the 12-year-old's curiosity may be overstimulated."

All the controversy got Elvis his first screen test, on April 1, 1956, with Paramount. His audition of a scene from *The Rainmaker* was amateurish but good enough to land him a three-picture deal worth about a half-million dollars.

Three weeks later, Elvis made his first Las Vegas foray. Ironically, this glitzy town that would nurture Elvis' comeback a decade later was disheartening the first time around. Instead of the screaming teens that were Elvis' adoring supporters, the New Frontier Hotel was filled with their blue-haired moms and disapproving dads. Curiosity was probably the most positive emotion they felt toward the long-haired, hip-thrusting performer. Their response was so lackluster, even hostile, that Elvis' name was quietly dropped lower and smaller on the marquee, until Colonel Parker and hotel management agreed to tear up the two-week contract halfway through.

For consolation, Elvis had his booming record sales and two months later another hard-driving session at RCA studios, where he sailed happily into pure pop terrain with "Don't Be Cruel," backed by "Hound Dog." The disk was a huge success, although putting two potential smashes on one record cost Elvis a lot in lost sales. Fans could thank RCA's inexperience with the pop world and its attitude of "grab-it-while-he's-hot" for the bargain of two hits for the price of one.

In the studio, Elvis was as original and natural as he was on stage. His musical talents included grasping a song's melody and often the lyrics as well, after just one hearing. He pioneered an instinctive approach to music that the pop world uses now as a matter of course and was the first pop star to really produce his own material. Elvis improvised arrangements as he went, then performed up to 60 takes on a given song until it had just the right feel.

By summer's end, Elvis was in Hollywood to film *Love Me Tender.* Paramount turned it into a musical by adding four songs, including the title one, after Elvis was added to the cast. RCA couldn't fail with this record release: The company received 856,327 orders before shipping a single one.

The young country boy brought a lot of enthusiasm and hope with him to Hollywood, and it comes through in his first film. Although teenagers were disappointed that *Love Me Tender* was a Western, not a rock 'n roll vehicle, they came in droves, enabling it to recoup its million-dollar costs within three weeks—a record at the time. Every theater in the land filled with screams as Elvis poured on his wonderfully sweet, unself-conscious smile. Elvis was very much himself: affectionate, handsome, shy, and sexy to the core. Although he didn't play the starring role in *Love Me Tender,* it was arguably his most compelling acting turn in more than two dozen leading screen roles. He gave the kind of natural performance that lent credibility to his dream, often expressed, of becoming the next James Dean.

Elvis longed to be a movie star, to use the rock 'n roll fame as the vehicle to bring him there. In those heady days, anything seemed possible. Serious acting wasn't the only desire about which Elvis spoke openly. He made no secret about his first Hollywood crush, on leading lady Debra Paget. He confided his unrequited affections to a few Tinsel Town reporters and in long conversations with Gladys, his lifelong confidante. He even asked Debra to marry him, by long-distance telephone from Texas.

But Debbie Paget—who rejected the newcomer as a hayseed—was just the first in a long line of starlets whose names would be linked with Elvis', from Natalie Wood to Nancy Sinatra to Ann-Margret.

There was one girl who did have Elvis' heart, and gave him hers, too. Memphis native Anita Wood met the town's leading citizen in 1957, and they stayed a steady item until Priscilla appeared on the scene five years later. Anita was petite, curvaceous, and talented, a pop singer and dancer struggling through the local stage-and-television circuit to break into big-time show business.

Anita was the Girl Back Home, both to Elvis and to the fan magazines. Yet she was forbidden to be candid about her role in Elvis' life. Marriage, deemed Colonel Parker, was out of the question. "We could not publicly admit that we liked one another or were going together," Anita says. "I always had to say that we were just friends because otherwise the publicity would hurt his image. He had to be free so that all the girls, the fans, could love him."

Once his national career began, success came fast and with a big, big bang. From August to December 1956, Elvis monopolized the airwaves with three number one hits. "All Shook Up" spent eight weeks at the top of *Billboard's* Hot 100 chart. His next two movies, *Loving You* and *Jailhouse Rock,* were produced and released within a year of the distribution of *Love Me Tender,* and Elvis was back in Hollywood to begin work on *King Creole.* He toured Canada and made a third appearance on Ed Sullivan. The income rolling in enabled him to give Gladys a pink Cadillac and to buy Graceland, where he established the Presley family compound.

He purchased the estate in March 1957 from a local Memphis family for $100,000, and he made it his home for the next 20 years. It became a Mecca for the King's millions of fans. Many photographs on these pages were snapped outside the estate's wrought-iron music gates, where admirers congregated for hours in the hope of getting a glimpse, a photo, or maybe even a word with Elvis. Such was the King's drawing power that when police anywhere in the United States were alerted of a female teenage runaway, they contacted Memphis first to check the throng outside the gate. Elvis was on top of the world, both personally and professionally.

Then, on December 20, 1957, he received a personal visit from the chairman of the Memphis draft board. He'd brought an induction notice for Elvis. Of all the boys in Memphis, why him? Why then?

Some suspect that powerful people wanted to get him out of the way: the forces of suburban complacency reasserting themselves. After all, Elvis was doing much more than inventing an art form: He had unleashed the passion of a generation and had redefined its relationship to music and dance, its attitude toward fashion and most of all, toward propriety. It was too late to push all that back in the box, but timid, conservative America was prepared to try. A draft certainly would get Elvis out of the way, at least for a couple of years, giving things a chance to settle down.

It worked. The meteor would shortly flame out, halfway across the sky. And a Memphis boy whose only crime was an uncontrollable wiggle on stage would pass many sleepless nights wondering when he'd have to go and whether his fans would remember him in his absence.

Opposite page: Elvis, age 9, at Lauderdale Courts, where the Presleys lived until Gladys' $4-a-day nurse's aide job meant eviction from public housing. The photo at right was Gladys' favorite.

Elvis had to borrow a bicycle—his parents had bought him a guitar instead.

Elvis is in the top-right corner, wearing overalls. He attended sixth grade in Milam School, Tupelo, Mississippi, after moving from East Tupelo, where he went to Lawhon Elementary.

Fifteen-year-old Elvis with friends.

With his fellow school library workers, Elvis is in the top-right corner.

Hanging out with friends, Elvis has already adopted a pompadour and jive style of dress.

Humes High School, Memphis, Class of 1953.

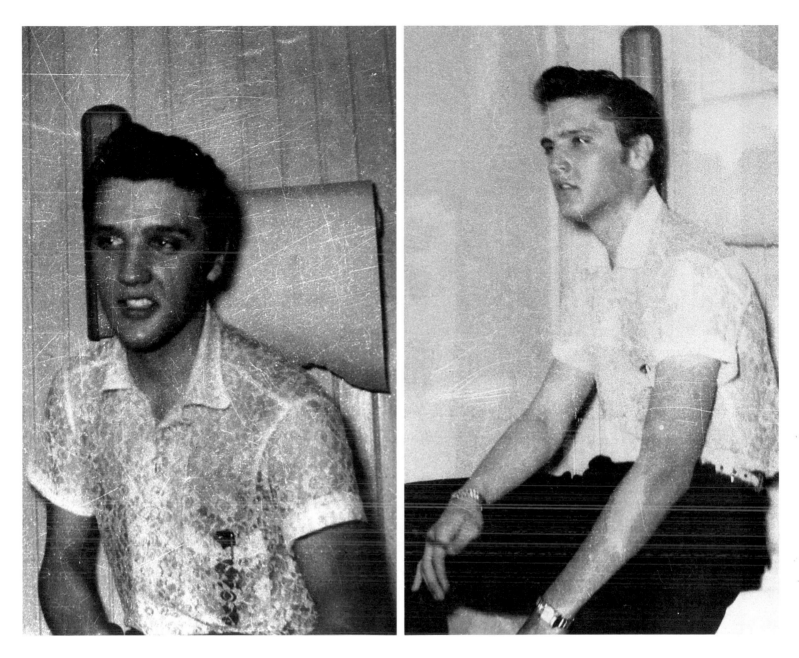

"I just relaxed and sang in my own style," said Elvis after his first recording session. The result was "That's All Right (Mama)," released in 1954, which had its first airplay on WHBQ, a white station that played songs by black bluesmen.

Opposite page: These photos were taken during Elvis' earliest barn-storming years. Clockwise from upper left: posing with a fan; outside the Eagle's Nest Club, where Elvis covered Dean Martin hits between big band sets; with a fan while on tour with Bill Haley and the Comets; snapped at the time Elvis was recording on the Sun label.

Elvis' early wardrobe ranged from bow ties to black lace shirts. He always had time for his fans and here is snapped tinkering with an accordion.

Opposite page: Elvis hugging super fan Jan Edwards, backstage, Richmond, Virginia, during the Hank Snow tour 1955.

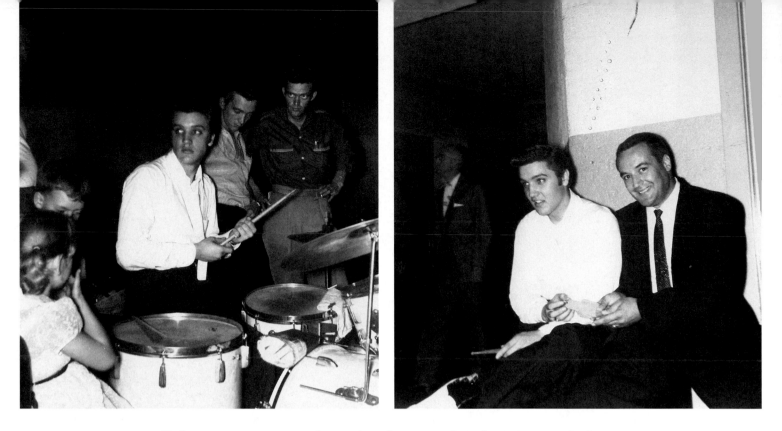

All shot in 1955, a pivotal year for Elvis. He played 200 gigs with the Blue Moon Boys, including tours of Nevada and numerous states through the South.

July 1956. Elvis was vacationing at the Gulf Hills Dude Ranch in Biloxi, Mississippi, when fans recognized him and asked for autographs.

These rare photos were taken in Tupelo, Mississippi, when Elvis returned for the 1956 centennial of his birthplace. Memphis contributed police officers to guard its adopted son.

Opposite page: Elvis taking a break from a grueling schedule at the Gulf Hills Dude Ranch in Biloxi, Mississippi, in July 1956.

Elvis with fans.

With his pink Cadillac in Shreveport, Louisiana, in 1956.

In front of Lansky's Men's Store, where Elvis bought his clothes for "a dollar down and a dollar paid every week." (1956)

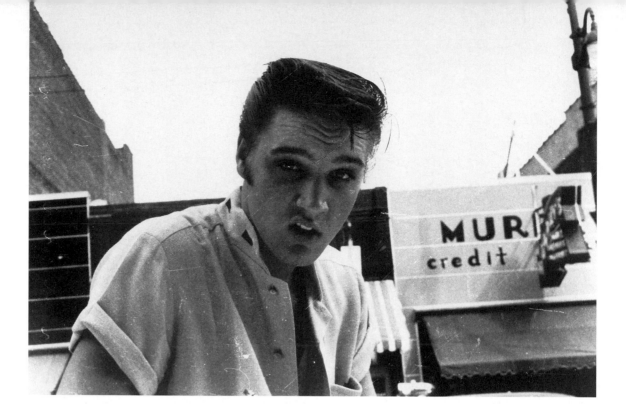

All taken in
Memphis in 1956.

Elvis at home.

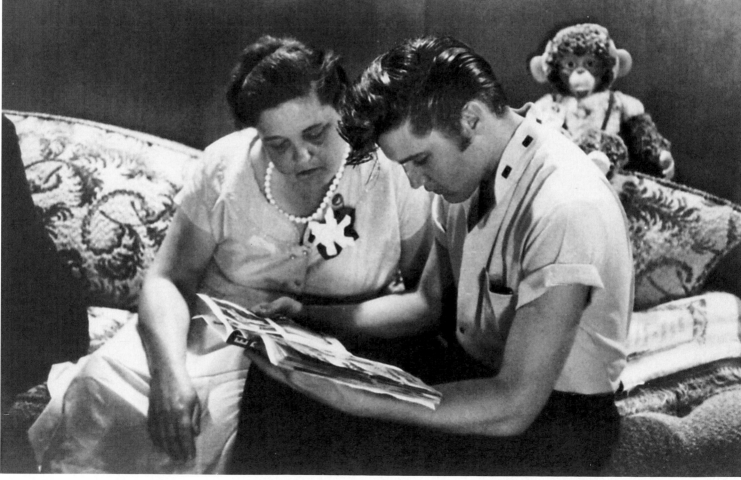

Elvis and his mom share a moment with an Elvis Presley fan magazine.

With three waitresses in Dallas.

With fans.

44

Backstage with fans following a 1956 performance.

Opposite page: Posing in front of the Presleys' new home on
Audubon Drive, Memphis.

April 1956 press conference at the Philadelphia Arena.

Posing outside WHBQ where the George Klein Radio Show was broadcast. (Memphis 1956)

Left, outside the house on Audubon Drive, Memphis. Below left, with Scotty Moore, stopping for gas while on tour. Below, outside Ellis Auditorium in February. (All photos 1956)

Arriving at Graceland. (1956)

Opposite page: Two photos at top, "Win A Date With Elvis" Contest winner—Andrea June Stephens from Atlanta, Georgia 1956.

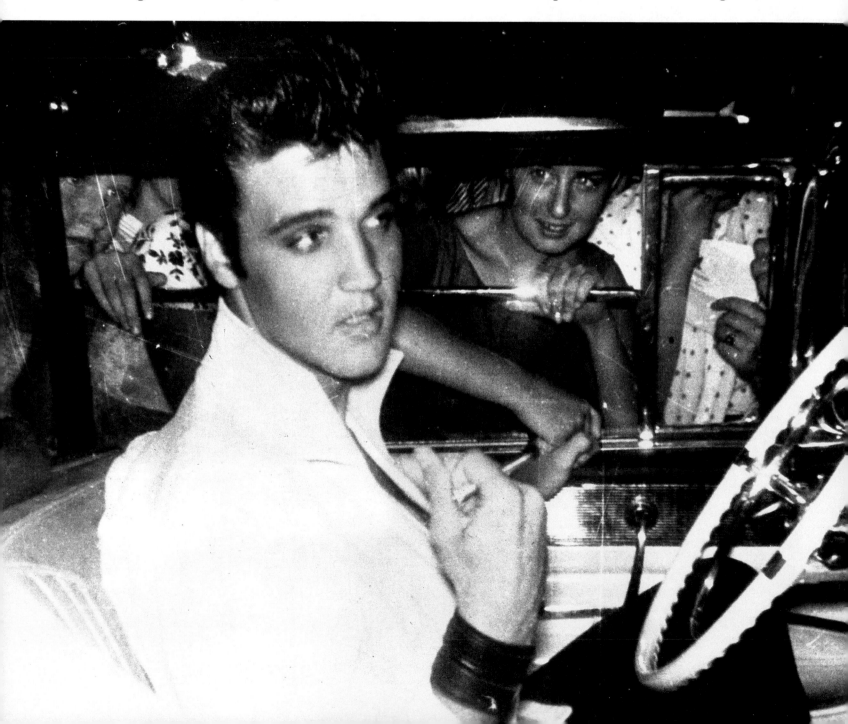

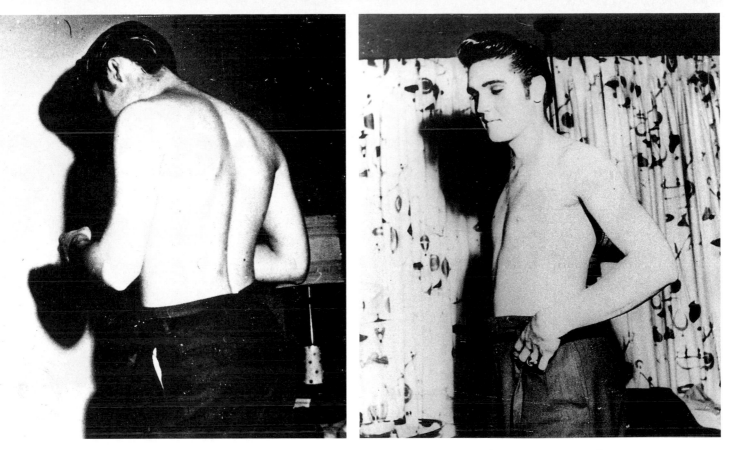

All of these shots were taken in Elvis' private suite at the Frontier Hotel, Las Vegas. After breakfast, he would read fan mail while playing records. (1956)

Opposite page: Taking a break during a "Love Me Tender" recording session. (1956)

The photos on these pages were taken in April 1956 at the Frontier Hotel, Las Vegas. Unfortunately, Elvis didn't get to perform for these fans but put on his show for their stodgy parents, who did not swoon for the entertainer that the hotel billed as "atomic-powered."

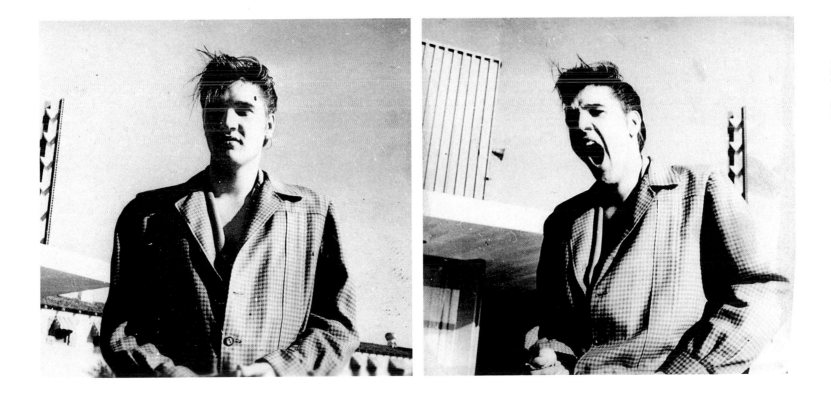

Mingling with the fans at the Frontier Hotel.

Elvis plays the piano for fan Judy Spreckles.

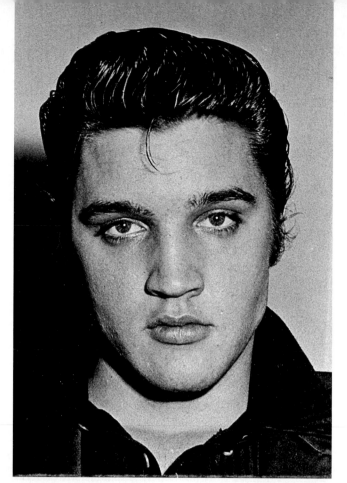

1956 mug shots.

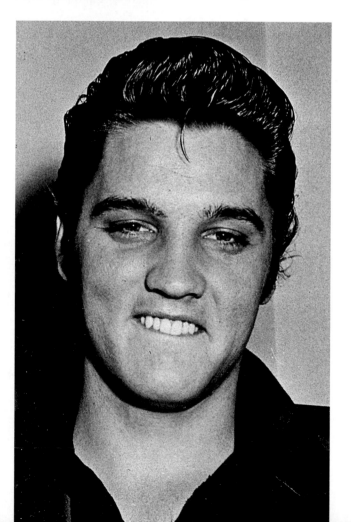

58

At the end of the Frontier Hotel gig.

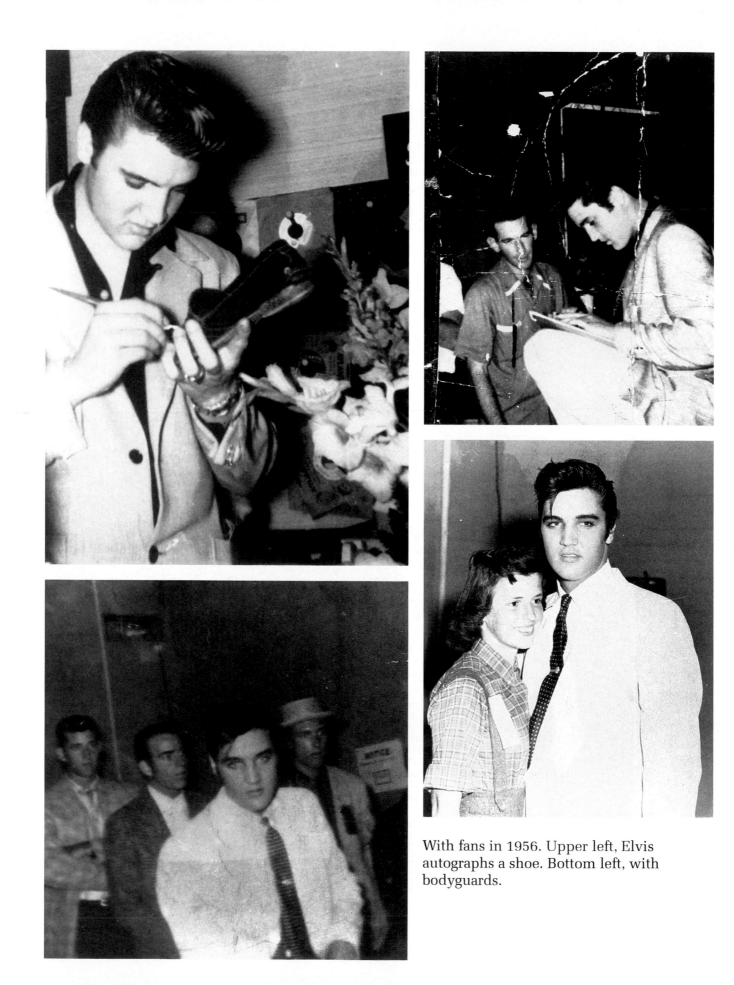

With fans in 1956. Upper left, Elvis autographs a shoe. Bottom left, with bodyguards.

With fans.

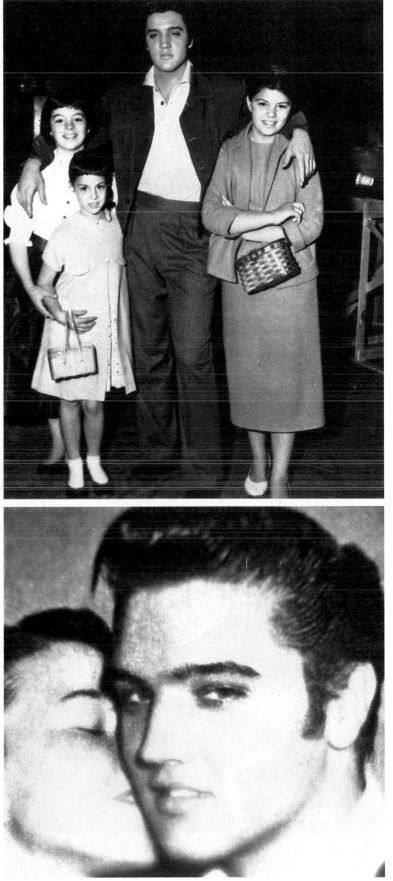

With Anita Wood.

A fan kisses Elvis for winning his
court case alleging assault of a
gas station attendant. (1956)

Elvis makes a personal appearance at a record store in San Diego, California the day after the Milton Berle Show.

The King relaxes. (1956)

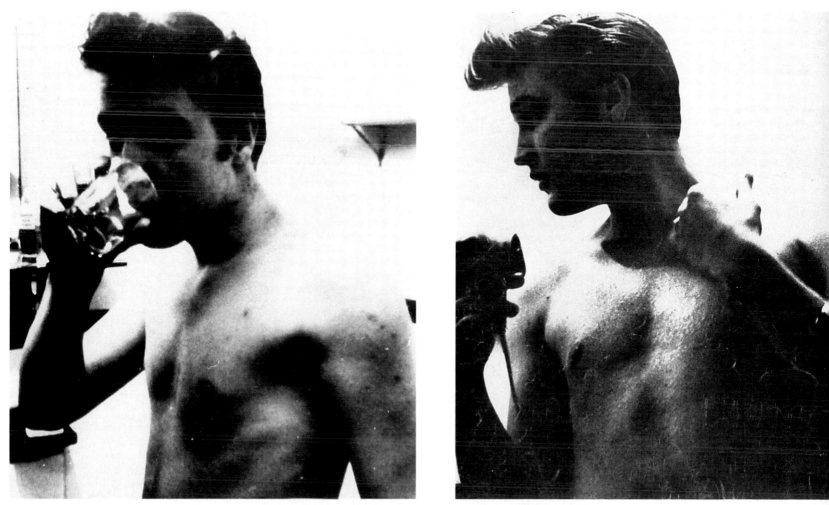

Morning ablutions. (1956)

With girlfriend Kate Wheeler in Dallas.

Captured after
a business meeting.
(1956)

Elvis already owns
his horseshoe ring,
one of his favorites.

Opposite page: In his '56 convertible.

Aboard the *Matsonia* en route to Hawaii. Elvis took a liking to these children and spent the whole day with them. (1957)

All the photos on these pages were taken in 1957, about the time Elvis was making *Loving You*.

Autographing an Elvis Presley skirt.

Opposite page: Standing in an empty room inside Graceland. (1957)

Elvis with fans outside the gates of Graceland. (1957)

70

These two photos capture Elvis with fans during his only Canadian tour.
The one at the bottom shows him with a fan in Ottawa after the April 3
concert. He's wearing his $10,000 gold lamé suit. (1957)

Opposite page: Elvis jokingly stole a cigarette from a fan before posing for this picture. (1957)

Opposite page: Upper left, Elvis relaxes. Upper right, with a fan in Tupelo, Mississippi, on October 3. Below, back in Memphis, driving one of his many cars. Elvis had a special fondness for convertibles. (All photos 1957)

Elvis and best friend George Klein, escorted by police while touring Canada. (1957)

Horseback riding at Graceland. (1957)

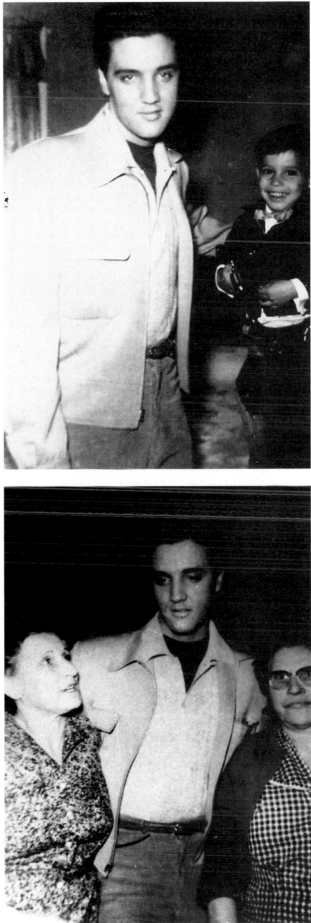

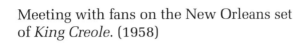
Meeting with fans on the New Orleans set of *King Creole.* (1958)

Opposite page: On the back steps at Graceland. Elvis' rock 'n roll years are drawing to a close with the decade. (1958)

While in New Orleans for the filming of *King Creole*, Elvis accepted an invitation to the home of some fans. (1958)

The Presleys plus a friendly fan on a family fishing trip on the *Aunt Jennie*. (1958)

Shortly before putting down his microphone to pick up a gun as a private in the U.S. Army. (1958)

THE

ARMY

The visit from Memphis draft board president Milton Bowers was not unexpected. Nearly a year before, on January 4, 1957, Elvis had reported for his preinduction physical at a Memphis veterans' hospital. Unlike the usual recruit, who moves through the day with about 40 others, Elvis went it alone—relatively speaking, that is, given the hordes of fans, journalists, and photographers trying to grab a shot of the King with his robes off.

On January 8, Elvis' 22nd birthday, the Army recruiters held a press conference to pronounce Elvis "A-profile," the highest physical category. The Army spokesman declined to release either his actual score or the date Elvis might be drafted. That would depend, he said, on such factors as the Memphis quota and the number of local volunteers. Once he was called up, Elvis would get to select the branch of service he would like to enter.

The nation's teenagers bit their nails, awaiting word of Elvis' draft. But there could be no doldrums where the King was concerned. A tempest was still swirling around a published story that quoted unnamed Army sources as assuring that Private Presley would receive preferential treatment: hair left long, time off to record and make films, an abbreviated basic training period. The hint had surfaced first in *Billboard,* dateline Fort Dix, New Jersey, around the time of Elvis' physical, but other publications picked it up over time, including the *Associated Press.*

"Relax, girls!" was the AP piece's jovial beginning. Many readers did not. The notion of star treatment for Elvis unleashed an immediate uproar, particularly from veterans. Some even complained to their Senator, who made a formal inquiry to the Pentagon. The Pentagon issued an immediate response denying the article and blaming its allegations on the circus that had surrounded Elvis' physical: "Many were present and it is possible that numerous conjecturable remarks and off-the-cuff comments were expressed by military personnel, cameramen and reporters. It must be emphasized that these remarks, if made, do not represent the official position of the Department of the Army."

If drafted, Elvis would be inducted at Fort Chaffee, Arkansas. Post spokesman Captain John Mawn further squashed any lingering rumors. "No one gets preferential treatment at Chaffee. All recruits get a military haircut the day they arrive." It was not unlike, he added, "a peeled onion."

The storm continued to rage. On one side, groups like the Veterans of Foreign Wars raised a ruckus in the press and with their legislators. Kentucky state representative Nick Johnson resigned from his draft board, saying, "I cannot conscientiously ask any mountain boy to serve the same country unless afforded the same treatment as Presley." On the other side, fans were furious with the Memphis draft board, calling Milton Bowers around the clock, even threatening him. "I'm fed to the teeth," he said. "I talk Elvis Presley more than I sleep. With all due respect to Elvis, who's a nice boy, we've drafted people who are far, far more important than he is. After all, when you take him out of the entertainment business, what have you got left? A truck driver."

When you reflect upon it, why *shouldn't* Elvis have been funneled into Special Services? There was no war in the late '50s. Elvis' talents would have been much better used to burnish Uncle Sam's image for potential volunteers; revving up the troops and selling bonds with his songs and smile would have been more effective and more fun than plugging along as just plain serial number US53310761. But the articles made such an assignment politically impossible.

Who planted the story? The Pentagon denied it. So did the Memphis draft board. An ambitious reporter? *Billboard* attributed its information to unnamed business associates of Elvis. For many, that points the finger squarely at Colonel Parker. But if so, why? One school of

thought holds that he wanted to cut Elvis down to size, to make him remember who had put him in the spotlight and that, furthermore, the Colonel couldn't stomach the concept of Elvis performing free—even for Uncle Sam. Another school believes it wasn't malice, just bad advice on how Elvis should change his black-leather image to that of red-blooded All-American. Whether Parker engineered Elvis' having been drafted in the first place or not, he did see Elvis' service as a public relations plus and milked it for all it was worth. Unfortunately, it was no game for Elvis: He was the one who had to live through the experience. The very prospect of Army service terrified him, and the reality would prove both personally debilitating and damaging to his career.

By the time the induction notice came, Elvis was, if nothing else, resigned. "I'm kinda proud of it," he told reporters. "It's a duty I've got to fill and I'm gonna do it."

Paramount Pictures, however, felt differently. Filming on *King Creole* was supposed to begin the same week as Elvis' basic training, and the studio stood to lose as much as $350,000 if their star didn't show. Elvis requested a deferment, which the Memphis draft board unanimously granted. With a new induction date of March 20, 1958, Elvis thanked the board and headed to Los Angeles to make his last pre-Army film.

King Creole was Elvis' fourth and favorite movie. It was also his first to be shot on location—the French Quarter of New Orleans. Cast, crew, and entourage relocated there after finishing the studio work in Hollywood, struggling with the screaming presence of the hundreds of fans who thronged the set. In the film, Elvis plays a busboy-singer in a New Orleans cabaret, where he falls in with small-time hoodlums and agrees to help them rob his father's store. Luckily, he meets a sweet store clerk (Dolores Hart) who helps him back to the straight and narrow and a reconciliation with his father. Along the way, he sings 11 songs, which RCA promptly released as singles, EPs, and LPs, a number of which sold over a million.

It was raining at 6:30 A.M. on March 24, 1958 when Elvis arrived at the Memphis draft board, straight from an all-night send-off at Graceland. A crowd of at least 50 journalists and photographers were waiting, along with swarms of fans and even Colonel Parker, who was handing out "See *King Creole*" balloons. The swarm from the media bulged to around 200 by midday. Elvis and a hapless dozen other recruits endured the poking and prodding that constitutes induction day illuminated by a thousand popping flashbulbs.

The circus went on all day. In the afternoon, the Colonel announced an impromptu news conference and got the cameras to roll as Elvis read telegrams, such as Tennessee Governor Frank Clement's: "You have shown that you are an American citizen first, a Tennessee volunteer, and a young man willing to serve his country when called upon to do so." The following day, young fans followed the bus that took Elvis to Fort Chaffee, and even sneaked into the barracks. The media trailed Elvis into the long-anticipated barbershop, where he wanly joked, "Hair today, gone tomorrow" as thousands of photos captured every angle of the most famous haircut in modern history.

Elvis paid his 65 cents, then dashed to a phone booth to call Graceland, but Gladys was unable to come to the phone. She was in bed, "grieving," he was told. It made Elvis' induction the first life experience that he—a sensitive only child—had been unable to share with his mother. The day also marked the start of Gladys' physical and emotional decline. We can imagine Elvis' pang of loneliness as he stood in a phone booth, only the smudged glass affording him a moment's privacy from the hordes of hungry photographers.

Elvis was looking at another potential abyss from that phone booth—the one he feared might swallow up his professional success. There's no time off for good behavior in the Army, which meant Elvis stood on the threshold of a two-year interruption in a career that had been powered by astonishing momentum. Two years is a long time in the pop world. And while Elvis might have helped invent rock 'n roll and remained its acknowledged king, a slew of pretenders would launch plenty of product in their battle to unseat him. With no new movies, records, or concert tours, Elvis would be helpless to defend his title.

From Fort Chaffee it was on to Fort Hood, Texas. Elvis was assigned to A Company, Second Medium Tank Battalion, Third Armored Division. He did well on all his aptitude tests, though not well enough to qualify for the Officers Candidate Exam. He rose promptly, and his zealous participation in the competitive training exercises won him praise from his drill instructor and an appointment as assistant squadron leader. When his efforts on the pistol range fell below standard, he took a remedial course in his time off.

In short, Elvis was a perfectly average G.I.— no ordinary feat given his constant scrutiny by the world media, Army brass, and fellow soldiers. Elvis was bravely swimming Army circles in a fishbowl, and a lot of people licked their whiskers as they waited to pounce on any blunder or sign of goldbricking.

Elvis gave no one that opportunity. Determination helped, as did a support system he built of Master Sergeant Bill Norwood, in whose home Elvis was a frequent guest; Eddie Fadal, a Waco cinema operator; and steady girlfriend Anita Wood, who traveled to Fort Hood nearly every weekend. After the first eight weeks, the clan arrived to add their reassuring presence, and Elvis installed Vernon, Gladys, and grandmother Minnie Mae in a three-bedroom house near the base. As they were technically his dependents, Army regulations permitted Elvis to sleep off-base with them. The family also planned to follow Elvis to Germany, which must have set his mind further at ease.

The summer began well in other ways, too. Elvis had lost 12 pounds in basic training and had hardened up. On June 10, he went to Nashville to record, just as a song from *King*

Creole, "Hard-Headed Woman," zipped to the top of three *Billboard* charts. *King Creole,* released at the same time, garnered the best reviews of any Elvis vehicle. *Billboard* gave kudos to Elvis' "best acting performance to date"; *Hollywood Reporter* said Elvis showed real promise; and longstanding critic Howard Thompson of *The New York Times* wrote, "Elvis Presley can act . . . [that's] his assignment in this shrewdly upholstered showcase, and he does it."

But things changed. Gladys' health must have been troubling her long before she told anyone about it, but by August she looked and felt poor. She was having trouble walking and concentrating and was slipping into a constant gloom enlivened only by bursts of temper. She was also drinking. Elvis and Vernon finally insisted she return home to Memphis to see the family doctor, who immediately admitted her to a private room in the brand-new Methodist Hospital. The diagnosis: hepatitis.

Her condition was serious. Elvis, frantic, stayed in constant touch with her doctors from Fort Hood while he fought for an emergency leave. Gladys' life was fading away. Finally granted leave, Elvis contradicted his mother's wishes and boarded a plane to her bedside, where he and Vernon kept a constant vigil.

Her death several days later—officially listed as a heart attack, although the family refused an autopsy—devastated Elvis. He sobbed for days, putting any energy that wasn't absorbed by his wracking grief into preparing an elaborate funeral. Arrangements were made to fly in the Blackwoods, Gladys' favorite gospel group. Vernon wanted a huge funeral at Graceland, with loudspeakers on the lawn to allow everyone to hear the singing and preaching. Soon, though, the crowd of well-wishers grew out of hand. They ranged from distant Presley relatives up from Mississippi to fans to women bringing covered dishes of food, in the rural southern tradition. Some women probably even thought of attracting Vernon's eye.

When Colonel Parker arrived, he saw Grace-land virtually under siege by the crowd and stepped in to rescue the grounds. He insisted the funeral be moved to a funeral parlor and fought with Vernon for hours to convince him. Vernon finally agreed and scheduled services for the next day. Over 400 people attended the funeral, which ran long, with the Blackwoods honoring request after request from Elvis and Vernon. As the cortege wound its way afterward to Forest Hill Cemetery, thousands of fans stood in respectful silence, lining a route patrolled by 150 uniformed police officers.

Elvis' emergency leave was extended one more week. Then, on August 24, 1958, he made his way back to Fort Hood in preparation for embarking with his unit to Germany. In Dallas, he spoke to reporters: "One of the last things Mom said was that Dad and I should always be together," he told them. "I'll report back to Fort Hood in the morning. Wherever they send me, Dad will go, too."

Elvis landed with his unit in Bremerhaven, Germany, on October 1 and immediately boarded a train to an Army base outside Friedberg, near Frankfurt in central Germany. Large numbers of photographs exist from this period, thanks to Army photographers. The post also allowed a large international press corps free run of the place to chronicle Elvis' first days. Elvis' role in the NATO defense was driving a jeep. It was described by the Army as a job with greater responsibility than his original tank assignment, but the hours were long and the task pretty unexciting. One of the week's high points, no doubt, was mail call, which brought Private Presley as many as 10,000 pieces at a time.

If that wasn't enough to reassure Elvis that his fans still remembered and loved him, there were his record sales. With very little unreleased material around, RCA was reduced to reissuing old songs. By February 1959, there wasn't one Elvis single on the *Billboard* Hot 100—the first time there had been such an omission since 1956. Then in March, RCA dug up and released "A Fool Such As I" and "I Need Your Love Tonight." Together they sold a million records (Elvis' 19th consecutive one) and hit the number two and four spots on the pop chart. The last nuggets of unreleased material went out in June: "A Big Hunk o' Love" and "My Wish Came True." This record, too, sold over a million copies and flew to number one. "It's a tribute to his staying power that he continues on such a powerful level," producer Steve Sholes told reporters a month later. "And we don't sell his records on a guarantee basis, you know." He meant that, counter to the usual industry policy, record-store owners couldn't return unsold quantities of Elvis' records.

While Elvis' fan mail included frequent love notes from his Memphis sweetheart, Anita Wood, an important new figure entered his world in 1959. Priscilla Beaulieu would eventually edge out Anita and all other contenders to become the most important woman in his life since Gladys. Elvis met her through Airman Currie Grant, who bumped into the 14-year-old Priscilla in the Eagles Club for American service families in Wiesbaden and invited her to join him and his wife on a visit to Elvis.

Imagine how sweet Priscilla must have looked at that first meeting, wearing a sailor suit and practically too shy to speak. Elvis, enchanted, spent time chatting with her, and when he sat down at the piano, he addressed his songs to her.

Priscilla arrived in Elvis' life at just the right time. He was very lonely after losing Gladys, who had always been his trusted confidante. His universe had shifted into one that was all male, from the Army by day to his evenings with Vernon and the good ol' boys he'd imported and installed in the house in Bad Nauheim. Young as she was, Priscilla wasn't in any way threatening. She was a beautiful young lady offering unconditional admiration and eventually, love. As a genuine American teenager, Priscilla could even provide reassurance of his continuing popularity back home, thus helping to ease Elvis' constant worry about

losing his fans while overseas.

The two saw a great deal of each other. Priscilla wasn't intimidated by their 10-year age difference, but comported herself as Elvis' peer. One of the things he must have shared with her was his unhappiness over his father's short-lived mourning period. Vernon was seeing Dee Stanley, a young mother divorcing her Army sergeant husband, who moved into the Presley home before the divorce was complete. Considering how public Elvis' life was already and the risk of scandal he was courting by being involved with an underage girl, he couldn't have been happy about this added threat. Elvis did not attend their July 3, 1960 wedding in Huntsville, Alabama, claiming to be tied up in the filming of *G.I. Blues.*

On March 2, 1960, Elvis put this anxious, boring period behind him. He'd passed his last inspection, done his last drill, signed his last autographs outside the white picket fence at Goethestrasse 14. Elvis was going home.

His homecoming was grand. From the landing at McGuire Field in New Jersey to the 48-hour train ride in a private car to Memphis, thousands of loyal fans waited patiently to glimpse the King and add their joyous screams to his homecoming. There were other signs that Elvis' place as King of Rock 'n Roll had been preserved. RCA rang up one million orders for his new record—"Stuck on You" and "Fame and Fortune"—which had yet to be recorded. Frank Sinatra handed Elvis a $125,000 check to commit him to sing two songs on Sinatra's upcoming musical television special, one in a series sponsored by Timex. *Life* magazine wanted to splash his portrait on the cover, but scrapped the plan when Colonel Parker requested $25,000 for the privilege (he *did* offer to refund it if *Life's* newsstand sales that week didn't go up at least 35 percent).

Easing Elvis back into place, too, was the vacuum at the top of the pops. Richie Valens, Buddy Holly, and the Big Bopper had died the year before in a plane crash. Chuck Berry faced a jail sentence for transporting a minor across state lines for immoral purposes, and Jerry Lee Lewis had fallen from grace for much the same thing—with his underage cousin. Little Richard was a tax exile, and fellow former-Sun-artist Carl Perkins' career had derailed after a bad car accident. The rock world was all shook up by the payola scandal: Deejay Alan Freed resigned on-air from New York radio station WABC in November, 1959, one step ahead of public charges that he had accepted money from record labels to play their artists. The remaining performers still out there, attempting to fill Elvis' blue suede shoes, were the likes of Fabian, Frankie Avalon, Bobby Darin, and Ricky Nelson—pale imitations all.

Elvis surely breathed a sigh of relief once he realized the kingdom was still his. He had great things to look forward to: live performances, recording sessions, his acting career. The Army was safely behind him. If he had any thoughts on the era he was leaving behind, it was probably only one. It may only have been an image, that of a beautiful face in a crowd, a teenage girl with a grown-up's maturity, waving to Elvis as he boarded the DC-7 in Frankfurt. Priscilla had captured Elvis' heart, but their goodbye didn't break it. Her beau was used to getting what he wanted, and in the case of Priscilla, it was just a matter of time.

At 6:35 A.M. on March 24, 1958, Elvis was sworn in at
Local Board No. 86.

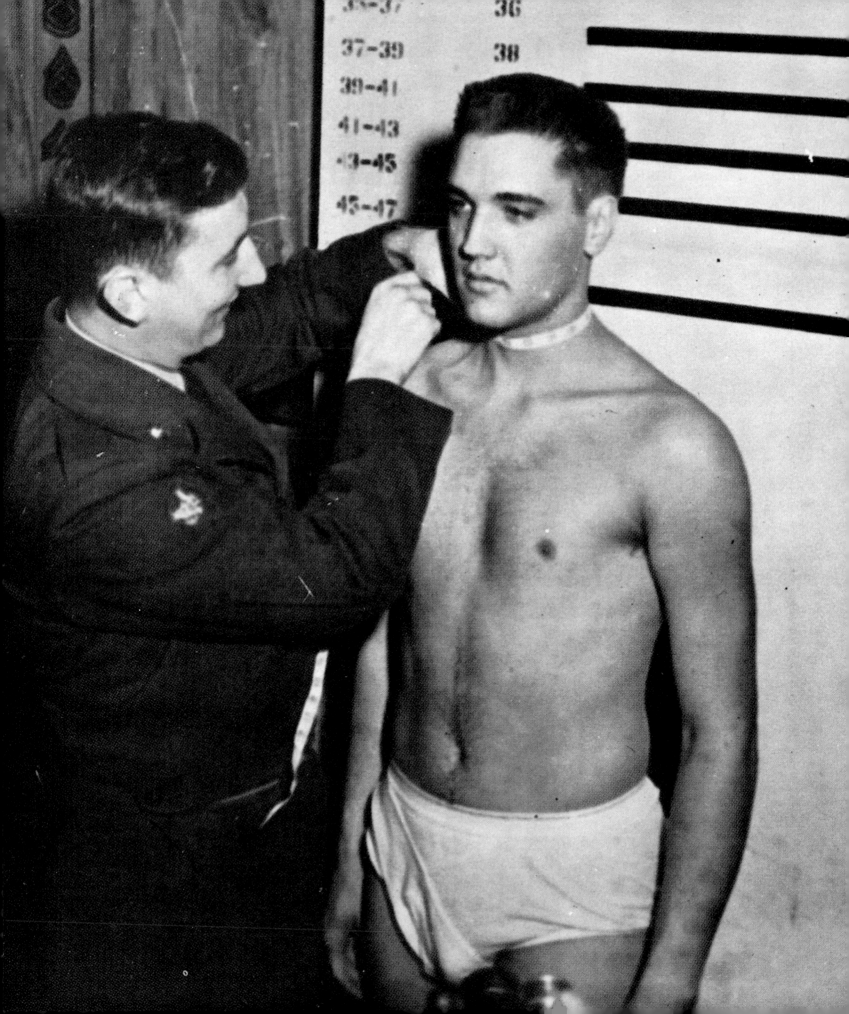

On January 4, 1957, Elvis reported for his preinduction physical, given by Dr. Leonard Glick at the Kennedy Veterans Hospital, Memphis.

Elvis' first Army dinner—spaghetti, salad, crackers, and two Cokes.

Opposite page: August 14, 1958, the day Gladys died. Her devoted son told friends he felt that everything he had was gone.

"Hell On Wheels" tank battalion, the Third Armor Division. Elvis is in the top row, third from left. In the close-up on the opposite page, the number 3 on his shoulder stood for the Third Armor Division. (1958)

Elvis had been made an acting assistant squad leader early in his basic training.

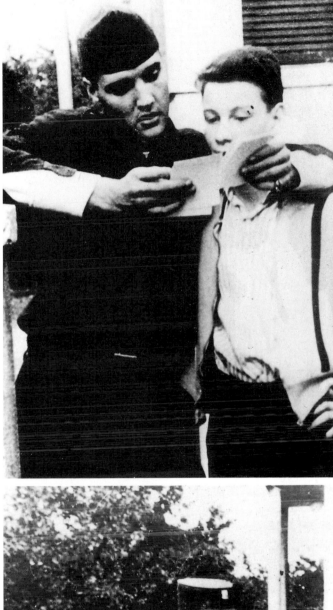

Upper left, with a young fan whose adoring letter so touched him that Elvis gave the boy a ring and had the boy spend the day with him.

Elvis was promoted to specialist 4th class on June 1, 1959. The honor also brought a raise, to $135.30 a month.

At the piano Elvis had installed in his house in Germany.

Opposite page: Priscilla Beaulieu was the daughter of a career U.S. Army officer living in Germany when she met Elvis.

In and around the house Elvis rented at 14 Goethestrasse in Bad Nauheim, Germany. A sign out front said, in German, "Autographs between 7 and 8 P.M. only!"

Surprised by some German fans, who said they learned English just for him.

Opposite page: Elvis at play and relaxing at his home off-base in Germany.

Taking a local young woman for a spin in his German sports car.

Elvis was frequently the center of attention during military parades and maneuvers.

Elvis at the home of the German "Win A Date" contest winners.

Opposite page: January 1958, the month Elvis was supposed to have entered the Army. The date was delayed until March, however, to allow Elvis to finish *King Creole*.

The good-natured star of the "Win a Date with Elvis" contest.

On January 20, 1960, Elvis was promoted to sergeant during winter field maneuvers in Grafenwohr, Germany.

On the way home to trade in his army cap for the crown he left behind.

Opposite page: Elvis being interviewed about the Army. Bottom: Elvis says goodbye to Army buddies.

HOLLYWOOD

The time Elvis spent fretting over his fans' loyalty proved groundless. His first week in America told him all he needed to know and set his mind at ease. Elvis was greeted like a king returning from exile.

While that must have been very gratifying in the short term, the long term effect is darker. The fans' kindness— their unconditional adoration—seems cruel or at least stifling, in retrospect. It seduced Elvis and corrupted him from his path of musical originality. After all, if the old formula worked so well, where was the motivation to try anything new?

It might have been good for Elvis to have had to fight his way back to the top—to prove himself once more. If the old crown hadn't been popped so quickly over his crewcut, he might have been forced to stretch himself in his film parts, to be more inventive in the recording studio, to woo his fans face to face once more on the concert circuit. At the same time, he would gain the greatest reward of all: inner satisfaction.

A long, luxurious train ride brought Elvis home from New Jersey to Memphis, with hundreds of fans screaming their welcomes at every whistle stop along the way. Once back at Graceland, he took two weeks out of the public eye to call old friends, reassemble the gang, consider some redecorating ideas, and just pad around the rooms and grounds he hadn't seen for 18 months.

On March 20, 1960, Elvis piled part of his entourage in the car and drove to Nashville for his first post-Army recording session. Many familiar faces were there: the Jordanaires, original band members Scotty Moore and D. J. Fontana, and studio musicians Buddy Harmon, Floyd Cramer, and Hank Garland. The only missing person was Bill Black, who had abandoned his spot in Elvis' band to become the leader of his own combo.

"Stuck on You," backed by "Fame and Fortune," was produced that night. RCA released the 45 rpm single before the month was out.

By April 25, it reached the top spot on *Billboard's* Hot 100 chart, where it stayed for four weeks (it also hit number six on the rhythm and blues list). The merchants who had helped the record ring up nonrefundable advance orders of more than 1,125,000 were not disappointed by their gamble. Pent-up Elvis fever ultimately generated the sale of more than two million copies.

Immediately after the recording session, Elvis boarded another train, this time to Miami, for the filming of Frank Sinatra's fourth and final Timex television special. In the history of people having to eat their words, Frank Sinatra earned a spot at the head of the table. Three years earlier, he had dismissed rock 'n roll as "phony and false, and sung, written and played for the most part by cretinous goons." Now, in an effort to boost his specials' lackluster ratings, he was hosting a rock singer—to the tune of $125,000—for three songs.

"Welcome Elvis" was an exercise in politeness. The two American entertainment kings got on like old friends. Despite his star billing, Elvis was his respectful self, donning a tux and calling his host Mr. Sinatra. He agreeably sang not only his two new singles but Sinatra's signature "Witchcraft." For his part, Sinatra seemed gracious about having passed on the role of teen heartthrob. Ol' Blue Eyes crooned his usual repertoire, plus "Love Me Tender." In the studio audience, two generations of idol worshippers swooned (the critics were less enthusiastic). Home viewers gave ABC a 41.5 share when it aired the special on May 12—nearly twice the ratings of its nearest competitor.

By April, RCA and Paramount were in a heated tug of war over who got the star first. Production had begun on *G.I. Blues,* cried Paramount's Hal Wallis, but record company executives were equally anxious to "fill the can" with fresh material. Elvis answered the musical call first, promising a speedy arrival in Hollywood as he headed back to Nashville.

One marathon, 12-hour session on April 4 produced enough material for an album, "Elvis Is Back," released one week later. On its heels, Elvis changed his musical direction with the single "It's Now or Never," released in July 1960.

"It's Now or Never," far more "romance" than rock, became Elvis' second post-Army hit. It stayed at number one for five weeks, thanks in part to airplay on a much broader spectrum of stations than usually played Elvis songs. In England, the cut stayed number one for eight solid weeks—setting the record for any Presley single in the United Kingdom.

Within three weeks of its U.S. release, "It's Now or Never" sold over 1,125,000 copies. The final tally was a phenomenal 22 million copies worldwide.

Into the can went "Are You Lonesome Tonight?" which RCA held to release in November 1960. By November 28, that single hit the top of *Billboard's* Hot 100 chart, where it stayed for six weeks, as well as numbers 22 and 3 on the country and rhythm and blues charts, respectively. Total sales exceeded four million copies.

In late June 1960, Elvis, with nine buddies, boarded a luxurious, private railroad car to Hollywood. In every sense, he left Nashville behind.

G.I. Blues disappointed everyone, except, probably, Colonel Parker, whose eyes rarely wandered from the bottom line. Indeed, the flick quickly grossed $4.3 million in North America alone, and its 11 songs comprised the Elvis LP album that spent the longest time on *Billboard's* Hot LP chart (111 weeks). Ten of those weeks were at number one.

The story centered on one Tulsa McLean, an Army tank gunner stationed in Germany. Tulsa accepts a $300 bet with a fellow G.I. over who can score first with a sophisticated nightclub dancer (Juliet Prowse). Compared with the old, wildcat Elvis, this one—no sideburns, short hair, a uniform instead of black leather—wasn't much of a temptation. The filmmakers domesticate this denatured creature even further with a silly baby-tending scene. Who was this new Elvis?

The fans wanted to know, and so did the critics. "When they took the boy out of the country, they apparently took the country out of the boy," wrote the *Hollywood Reporter's* critic, Jim Powers. The picture, he concluded, would "have to depend on the loyalty of Presley fans to bail it out at the box office."

Elvis wanted to know himself. He hated *G.I. Blues* and came down hard on the Colonel to get him meatier film roles. He didn't want to become a cinematic cliché; he wanted to stretch himself as an actor. Many believe that serious cinema was Elvis' deepest desire. Rock 'n roll was merely to open Hollywood's door.

Dutifully, the Colonel wrangled with Twentieth Century Fox, Elvis' current studio. The next movie, *Flaming Star,* was set to begin filming in October. A compromise was reached. Elvis would sing four songs. That was down from the normal near-dozen, plus he'd play a dramatic role, that of a half-breed son of an Indian mother and white rancher in frontier America. There would be lots of gun slinging, horseback riding, emotional confronting.

The film that followed was another dramatic attempt, *Wild in the Country*. Writer Clifford Odets demonstrated that his reputation was, at that juncture, bigger than his talent. Fans and critics alike decried this turkey as a steamy, southern *Peyton Place*.

Unfortunately for Elvis' dramatic aspirations, neither film showed him off as a great acting talent, nor was either a box office smash. That fact especially gave strong ammunition to the Colonel, whose arguments for a shift to light comedy were backed by a Greek chorus of producers Hal Wallis and Hal Kanter and William Morris Agency president Abe Lastfogel. Many see the same forces at work here as those that drafted Elvis, then kept him out of Special Services. Forcing Elvis to abandon his dreams of being a dramatic actor was part of the same calculated effort to change his radical, danger-ously sexual image. It was an attempt to have Elvis taken less seriously.

The Colonel's part in this also had to do with his having a hard time believing that rock 'n roll would last. He wanted Elvis to have a cleaner-cut image that would broaden his appeal beyond the fickle tastes of rebellious, libidinous teenage girls.

Outgunned, Elvis agreed to make *Blue Hawaii*. It furthers the sanitization of Elvis that *G.I. Blues'* lost sideburns and black leather had begun. In it, his love interest, played by Joan Blackman, has all the sexual sizzle of a summer-camp volleyball game. At one point, Elvis paternally spanks a sassy teen. If that isn't enough taming, the fatherly hero ends the movie at the wedding altar.

Blue Hawaii premiered in November 1961 and became Elvis' greatest commercial film success. If Elvis hadn't been pushed to do so many movies, one after the other, he might have waited for roles that made him push himself instead of playing the same character over and over again. He might have found the time to study acting, much as Marilyn Monroe did. Perhaps if he'd been surrounded by a genuine support system, he'd have gotten the encouragement at least to get a drama coach.

Meanwhile, the recording studio was quiet. "It's Now or Never" and "Are You Lonesome Tonight?" marked the end of Elvis' hit singles for 1960, at least in the United States. A few cuts off his albums were released in Europe, including "Wooden Heart," from *G.I. Blues,* which he sang partially in German and which sold a million copies there despite a government ban on its radio play.

Blue Hawaii set up the new formula: Elvis as beefcake, surrounded by sex kittens at a beautiful, lush, or otherwise arresting locale. Each plot offered some limp excuse to hang a guitar around Elvis' neck and get him to burst into song, backed by an unseen orchestra. Throughout the '60s, he produced an average of three films a year. Yet as the decade moved on, rousing seemingly everything in America, the only evidence of the revolution outside the Elvis film studio was the increasing raciness of the camera angles and the skimpiness of the costumes they captured.

A select roster of Elvis movie titles includes *Girls! Girls! Girls!, Fun in Acapulco,* and *Tickle Me* (this last described by *The New York Times* as "the silliest, feeblest, and dullest vehicle for the Memphis Wonder in a long time"). It must have been galling for a man who'd once hoped to inherit James Dean's dramatic, bad-boy mantle. Yet how could a man who began life as poor white trash walk away from a salary of a million dollars per picture? As he would sing years later in "Suspicious Minds," Elvis was "caught in a trap." He had neither the external support or the "right stuff" inside himself to walk out.

In a way, the pictures weren't the worst part of Elvis' Hollywood years. The music was. "Good Luck Charm," released in February 1962, stood as Elvis' last number one single until the end of the decade. Ever attentive to quantity, not quality, the Colonel decreed in 1964 that his star wasn't going to compete with himself any more and from that point forward would record nothing but movie soundtrack albums. Elvis Presley's marvelous two-and-a-third octave range, soulful feeling, and great skills, not only at phrasing and emoting a song but at arranging it, were now reduced to such throwaways as "One Boy, Two Little Girls" *(Kissin' Cousins)* and "Wheels on My Heels" *(Roustabout).*

Gone were the earnest blues of the Sun sessions, the intensity of *Jailhouse Rock,* the soulful ache of "Heartbreak Hotel"—in short, all the original stuff inside Elvis that he'd poured out during the earliest days and that had caused him to rise so swiftly to the top of the charts. Now, more than the music was different. Elvis-Gone-Hollywood *looked* much the same as the Man from Tennessee. The flashy clothes, erotic gestures, twisted grin, all were long familiar and hadn't changed, but they were growing some-

what practiced, premeditated. Underneath, the essence of Elvis was slipping away.

The Hollywood years were gravely disappointing professionally, but Elvis' life had its compensations. There was the money, for one thing. His fee eventually reached about a million dollars per picture, which was to say about half the film's budget. By the mid-'60s, his fee alone made him the best-paid actor in Hollywood. When you add to that number 50 percent of the movie's profits, Elvis was pulling in five or six million dollars a year. Even minus the Colonel's 25 percent, there was enough to let Elvis live comfortably in the style to which he had become accustomed—he and the small piece of the Memphis economy he supported. Elvis always kept quite a few people on salary, from Vernon and the uncles who'd once taught him a few guitar chords, now employed guarding the music gates, to employees, related and not, working in his office, home, and grounds. There were also always members of the "Memphis Mafia" around, who were also known collectively as "the Guys." A partial list includes Joe Esposito, Lamar Fike, Marty Lasker, Charlie Hodge, Sonny West, Red West, Gene Smith, Billy Smith, Jerry Schilling, Alan Fortas, George Klein, Ray Sitton, Marvin Gamble, Jimmy Kingsley, Bitsy Mott, Patsy Gamble, and Cliff Gleaves. They were his 24-hour-a-day cronies whose tasks ranged from bodyguard to driver to companion. At one point, in 1965, Elvis' payroll included ten "Guys," three maids/cooks, two secretaries, three gatekeepers, and two yard men.

Another compensation was feminine attention. Never mind the adoring throngs—consider Elvis' leading ladies. Debra Paget, Nancy Sinatra, Natalie Wood, Ann-Margret—these were just some of the names linked with his during his many years in Hollywood. Which rumors were true? Elvis inspired discretion in his women.

Romantically, there was always the home-front. Elvis' relationship with Anita Wood continued on and off until 1961. The pert, loyal girl-next-door who often put aside her own show biz aspirations to be there for Elvis finally quit believing his promises of marriage "someday." With his next love interest already in the wings, Elvis had no reason to be too upset by Anita's departure.

That heartthrob, of course, was Priscilla. Since he left Germany in March 1960, Elvis telephoned her many times and received many letters, scrawled in her adolescent hand. Once Anita left the picture, Elvis wasted no time revving his engines for a full-speed assault on the Priscilla's parents. His first act was to convince them to let him fly their 14-year-old daughter to Graceland for the Christmas holidays that year.

For Priscilla, the visit was a dream. Elvis was openly devoted to her, and they spent long, lazy hours together. In a delicious change from the Bad Nauheim days, there was no rushing off at night in a car driven by one of the Guys to make her father's curfew. In fact, she ignored her promise to her parents that she would stay with Vernon and Dee and slept each night with Elvis at Graceland. Nonetheless, Elvis honored his private commitment to keep Priscilla a virgin. She remained so until their wedding night.

No sooner had Priscilla been returned safely to Germany than the lovers began plotting a permanent reunion. As any parent knows, the word "sullen" perfectly defines an adolescent denied. Priscilla sulked, refused to leave her room, and generally made Beaulieu family life miserable as she pressured her parents to let her move to Graceland.

Finally, they caved in. At the time Priscilla had neither educational nor career goals for her post-high school existence, and in a generation when most women were married by 21, the idea of a 16-year-old "encouraging" a fabulously wealthy entertainer who adored her—and with whom she was deeply in love—probably seemed more shrewd than strange. Priscilla

moved to Memphis in the spring of 1962, scattered enough possessions at Vernon and Dee's home to maintain appearances, and settled quietly into her classes at Immaculate Conception High School and long, social nights with the permanent hangers-on at Graceland.

Throughout the middle and late '60s, Elvis probably spent less time at Graceland than at his homes in Bel Air and Palm Springs. There he presided over endless parties involving him, the Guys, and dozens upon dozens of pretty girls. The Guys and Elvis played football without helmets and other games with an occasional violent twist, and there were assuredly some kinky scenes with the hordes of women willing to do anything for a night with or at least near Elvis. There may not have been open alcohol consumption, but Elvis was already caught up in the drug use that ultimately would contribute to his death.

Elvis made no public appearances from 1961 to 1967 and, following the Colonel's 1964 edict, cut songs only from his movies. He loathed these records and came to hate the movies, too. They were unreal, cookie-cutter vehicles, with 17-day shooting schedules that left no time to rehearse musical numbers or take pains to get anything else right.

Nobody else seemed to care. Producer Hal Wallis, whose 1964 work on *Becket* makes it clear that he was capable of quality, regarded Elvis as little more than leverage when he went to finance less commercial projects. The Colonel's fortunes rose with Elvis'—and he wasn't too interested in cultural enrichment. Priscilla, who was completely dependent on Elvis, rarely risked saying anything that might upset him. Nor did the Memphis Mafia.

Had Gladys lived, she might have talked to her boy and helped him find the strength to fight for better scripts or the time to make the ones he had better. But nobody ever replaced Gladys in Elvis' life, and the lessons she'd taught him—be polite, don't rock the boat, take care of the people who are financially dependent on you—blocked any stirrings he might have felt to fight for his growth as a performer.

Elvis was by now miles from his rock 'n roll roots. But something else had changed, too, something even deeper and more essential. His image and his inner self had reversed. He had begun public life as a teenage idol, with the look of a greaser and image of a sexual wildman, while underneath, he was safe—a gentle, courteous mama's boy. By the late '60s, his clean-cut looks and squeaky image had lost lots of teens but gained their blue-haired moms and even grand-moms. Behind closed doors, however, Elvis was not the wholesome guy he appeared. He had become the womanizing, rough-playing, drug-using tyrant he'd once portrayed. He no longer looked like a bad boy. He was one.

Elvis typically brought dates to the movies.

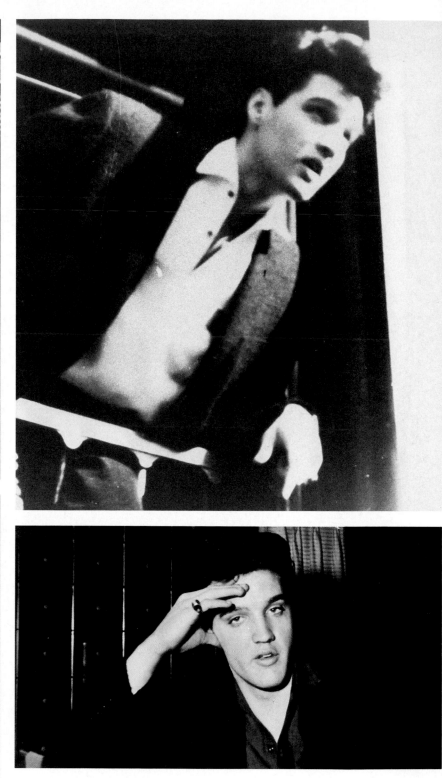

Above and opposite page, top, returning to Union Station, Memphis from shooting Frank Sinatra's Timex Special. (April 18, 1960)

Opposite page: Bottom left, at the Rainbow Skating Rink that Elvis rented for a party from 12 A.M. to 5 A.M. Bottom right: taking Anita Wood for a spin in "Dodgem Cars," Elvis' favorite ride at the Memphis Fairgrounds. (1960)

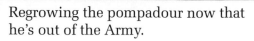

Regrowing the pompadour now that he's out of the Army.

On the set of *G.I. Blues*, where the winner of the third contest to meet Elvis was announced.

Top, in a Memphis official's office. Above, greeting a fan while filming *Wild in the Country*.

Opposite page: A lunch break—all the milks are Elvis'—between shooting scenes of *Flaming Star*. Elvis played an Indian and wore brown contact lenses to match his darkened skin. (All 1960)

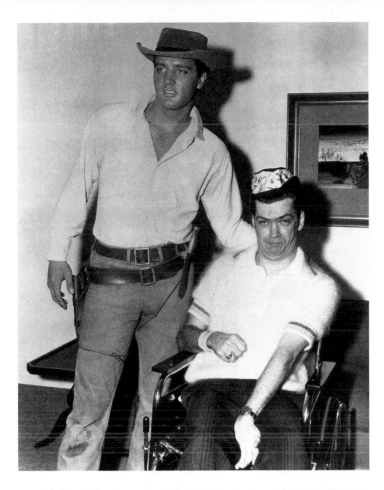

Above, with a fan on the set of *Girls, Girls, Girls.* Left, with Tankers fan club president, Gary Pepper on the set of *Flaming Star.*

Though Elvis loved the water and would swim and dive for hours, he was also hydrophobic, and insisted on having lots of people with him whenever he entered any body of water.

Elvis enjoyed football during the early '60s and sponsored a team, the E. P. Enterprises. Players included his friends and bodyguards Sonny West (middle row, left) and Red West (middle row, second from right). Elvis is in the top row, second from left.

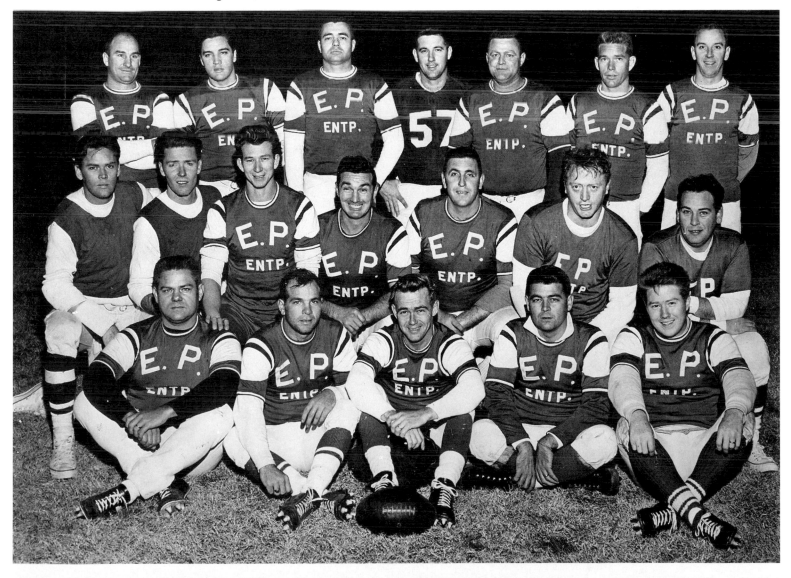

Near the end of filming *Follow That Dream*. Elvis is shown with Colonel Parker and swarms of fans. (1961)

Opposite page: Displaying a "wrist lock"—a judo/karate move that can break an arm—on the set of *Follow That Dream*.

With stagehands on the Florida set of *Follow That Dream.* (1961)

Elvis virtually commuted between Memphis and Hollywood. Here he is shown on the set of of *Kid Galahad* and, below, taking time to thrill this young fan. (All 1962)

Opposite page: The top four photos were shot at the Memphis Fairgrounds. Bottom photos were taken on the set of *Girls, Girls, Girls.* (1962)

Right, getting off his custom-made bus (his right hand in a cast because of a broken finger); below right, greeting superfan Jimmy Velvet (center) with musician Bill Lynn looking on.

Opposite page: Elvis frequently rented Memphis movie theaters for all-night private viewings of numerous films. Here, with different fans and friends invited to watch the show. (1964)

Greeting fans, signing autographs and relaxing in the Memphis area between movies in the early 1960s.

Elvis practices karate techniques in his stocking feet.

Elvis with some of his youngest fans in 1966 (left, with Priscilla in the background), 1967 (above), and below, with a young Priscilla and stagehands on the set of *Roustabout.*

Pictured far from the movie set. Top left, sporting his new hairstyle, bangs instead of a curl; top right, in front of Graceland in his $50,000 Rolls Royce, which Elvis gave away one day because he scratched it; left, with Priscilla and one of the animals they both loved; above, with grandmother Minnie Mae Presley and Priscilla.

On the set of *Paradise Hawaiian Style*.

With Priscilla, her hair dyed blonde, Jerry Schilling and girlfriend, at Graceland's meditation gardens. (1966)

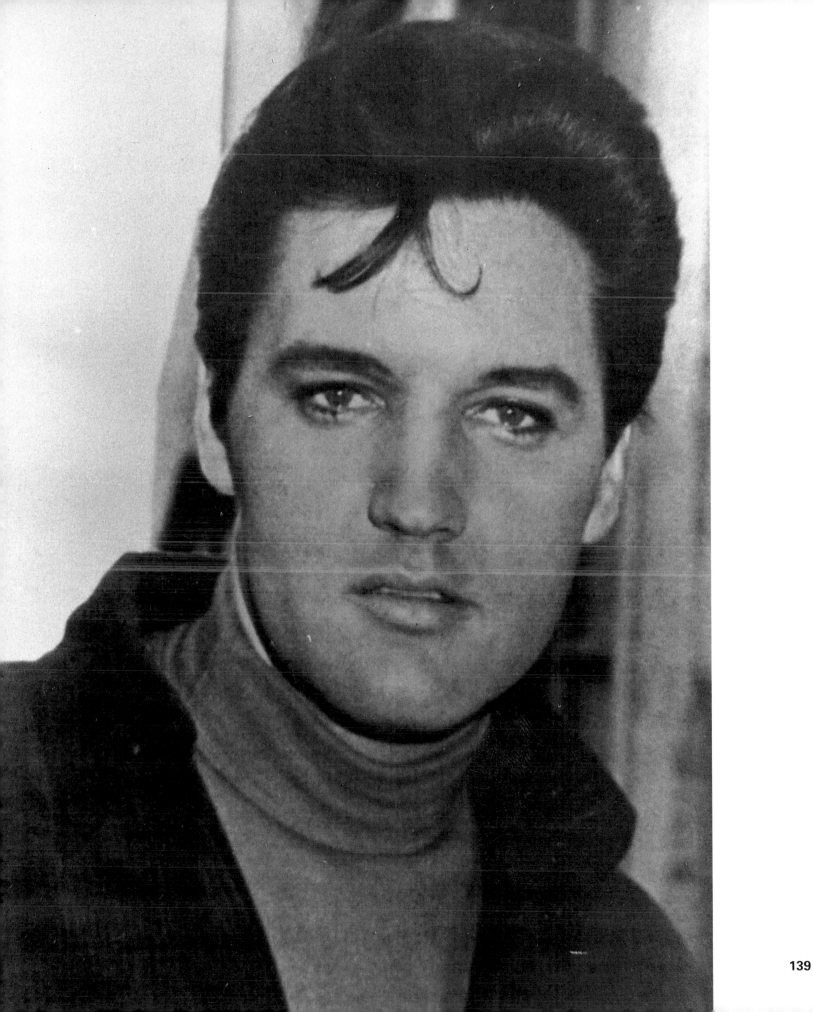

Inside the gates of Graceland during 1966. Top left, astride his
motorcycle; top right, with Tom Diskin, once Elvis' road manager; above
left, with Priscilla, Christmas 1967, backed by the life-size Nativity
scene Elvis commissioned; above right, a very rare photo of Elvis
standing on the grounds with a fan.

May 1, 1967. The song that was played for the bride was "Love Me Tender," but neither Presley had much to say about the rest of their Las Vegas wedding. Elvis didn't like Priscilla's gown, which he considered too plain.

Top left and right, the newlyweds in Palm Springs. Left and right above, water sports on their honeymoon.

Opposite page: With Priscilla on the third day of their Hawaiian honeymoon.

Above left, Christmas 1967 at his $500,000 Circle G Ranch in Walls, Mississippi. Above right and below, on the *Speedway* set with friends, including Nancy Sinatra, Dee and Vernon Presley, and the Stanley brothers. (1967)

On February 1, 1968, nine months to the day after their wedding, Priscilla gave birth to Lisa Marie.

At home with their newborn. Above, with grandfathers
Beaulieu (far left) and Presley (far right).

All photos taken at the Circle G Ranch during 1967 except for above right, on the Sedona, Arizona set of *Stay Away Joe*.

On the set of *Stay Away Joe* with co-star
Old Grey Mayer.

Elvis would ride his golf carts for hours around the Graceland grounds. A few years later, he taught Lisa Marie how to operate a cart of her own. (1968)

Top left, a fan brandishes her Kodak Instamatic. Top right, deeply tanned for *Stay Away Joe.* Above left, having lunch in Hawaii. Above right, taking a spin around the neighborhood in his dunebuggy. (1967)

On the set of *Live a Little, Love a Little*. Left, with Army buddies Charlie Hodge and Joe Esposito who replaced Tom Diskin when he retired as Elvis' road manager. (1968)

With fans. Top left, drinking Nesbitt, Elvis' favorite orange soda pop. Top right and opposite page, astride his horse, "Rising Sun." (1968)

Top left, a bearded Elvis for *Charro.* Above right, with superfan Judy Palmer on right. (1968)

At his Beverly Hills home, telling fans about new his movie, *Charro*.
Top left, with Blue Hawaiian Fan Club President Sue Wienhart. Below
right, in Arizona, on the *Charro* set. (August, 1968)

Top right, on the *Charro* set. All others, with fans and one of the many gifts bestowed upon Elvis outside his Beverly Hills estate. (1968)

Joking around with fans outside his Beverly Hills home, Elvis slants his eyes, greets superfan Sue Wienhart, and watches a fan do some karate moves. (1968)

On the set of *Trouble with Girls*. (1969)

Top, with one member each of a set of twins outside his Beverly Hills home. Above, an early shot of Elvis wearing a scarf and preparing his lines for that day's shooting schedule. (1968)

Top left, August 1968. Top right, around the time of the 1968 television special. Above right, May 1969, after completing *Trouble with Girls*. All outside his Beverly Hills home.

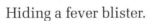
Hiding a fever blister.

Top left and right, Graceland, summer 1969.

In the spring of 1969, Elvis sported a Beatle haircut for *A Change of Habit,* his last feature film.

Reaching out to the fans gathered at Graceland and Beverly Hills, spring and summer, 1969.

Above, riding "Rising Sun". Below, the family with one of their dogs. Elvis bought Lisa Marie two Great Danes, "Brutus" and "Snoopy." (1969)

With little Lisa Marie.

LAS VEGAS

COMEBACK

Elvis turned 30 in 1965, in the midst of the massive upheaval and conflict that marked the '60s. Like many young Americans in that unsettled time, Elvis was often unsure of his proper direction.

Various contradictions characterized his life. Deep spiritual longings and ascetic quests coexisted with his impulsiveness and sexual curiosity—now expressed for real in wild parties at the Palm Springs house instead of pantomined on stage. The famous sex symbol was about to marry. A vulnerable, motherless child himself since Gladys' death, he chose a young bride to whom he could be both husband and father. He was dismayed by hippie culture, yet consumed more than his share of drugs. Though he had much cause for happiness in his life—and often was very content—he nevertheless spent many days tormented by doubt and depression.

Elvis entered his middle years at the peak of his success. His records sailed effortlessly up the charts, and his films made him Hollywood's highest-paid performer. He spent a decade proving the answer he gave to Sun Records' Marion Keisker in 1953, when asked who he sounded like: "Ma'am, I don't sound like nobody." Elvis was also beloved—not only by millions of fans worldwide but by friends, relatives, his leading ladies . . . and Priscilla. He worked hard, and played hard, too—whether riding his Harley Davidson or his horse Rising Sun, playing football or practicing karate, racing slot cars or renting an entire amusement park, roller rink, or movie house. There were always plenty of friends, relations, and hangers-on to accompany him on every adventure.

Yet depression and unhappiness darkened the spirits of Graceland's master. Elvis felt hopelessly out of control of his career. Though he was a box office smash, his success at light musicals blocked his heart's desire: to develop his talents as a serious actor. He continued to sing, but gave no concerts, he knew well that the numerous movie sound-tracks he cut in the mid-'60s were largely rubbish, but the Colonel forbade him to record anything else. Elvis was in some ways his own worst enemy, since he knew what to do to make himself happier yet never managed to do it.

What made this rich and famous King helpless? One factor was his own good manners, which made a fight with either the movie studios or Colonel Parker seem impossibly rude. It would have mocked his adored mother's upbringing. Elvis was not raised to question authority but to trust, obey, and respect it.

Money also played a factor in Elvis' unhappiness. He needed it to support not just a wife but an entourage. And so he was trapped making three films and dozens of songs that disgusted him every year—because his fear of being alone made having homes filled with friends not a luxury but a requirement. It was his protection against the loneliness that threatened to undo him—and ultimately did.

Had Elvis spent his life driving a truck for Crown Electric, he might have chafed sometimes at being stuck there for the sake of his family obligations. But fate took Elvis down a different path; his talent and originality brought him to stardom, and his artistry changed the sound of American pop culture. That *he* was trapped was more than galling—it was depressing and puzzling. Elvis couldn't figure out how this had happened to him. Since childhood, he'd felt he was meant to be and do something special.

From this bewilderment and disappointment was born Elvis' spiritual search. In April 1964, Elvis met Larry Geller, a barber who came to the Bel Air house to cut his hair. Geller was a California '60s prototype, a thin, laid-back hippie, into health food, meditation, and esoteric readings. As with everything else, from horseback riding (Elvis bought horses for the entire Memphis Mafia and their wives) to food (he ate the

same plateful of eggs and bacon every breakfast of his life), Elvis indulged to the hilt when he found something he liked. Geller became a key figure in his life for three years.

Under Geller's guidance, Elvis read dozens of books on the spiritual world, ranging from numerology to Rosicrucian cosmology to Far Eastern religious thought, from the 19th-century spiritualist charlatan Madame Blavatsky to the *Tibetan Book of the Dead*.

According to Priscilla, Elvis' long heart-to-hearts with Geller and discussions of these mysterious books left her feeling excluded and uncomfortable. She knew he was searching for answers to the fundamental questions that tormented him: Why was there so much pain and suffering in the world? Why had he been chosen out of the universe's multitudes of people to be so influential, and for what purpose could he best use that influence? And why, with so much in his life, wasn't he happy?

In 1965, Elvis discovered another guide in his search for enlightenment, Daya Mata (he fondly called her "Ma" for short), a California disciple of Yogi Paramahansa Yogananda. Though the yogi had died in 1952, his ashram still thrived on a serene hilltop above Pasadena. Elvis made frequent visits and financial contributions to this Self-Realization Fellowship.

Elvis' studies changed his normally playful personality. On movie sets, he no longer indulged in his famous practical jokes—he was too busy reading the spirituality books he toted back and forth each day. Back at Graceland, he remained devoted to his studies and even brought Geller home a few times. Elvis tried to involve Priscilla and the Guys in his quest for higher understanding.

Priscilla has said that he particularly pressured her, urging her to read the works that would help her to become his "soulmate." But the poor teenager could barely lift some of the thick tracts her sweetheart-mentor brought her, much less plow through them. Not only did he condemn her obvious lack of enthusiasm, but she reports that his spiritual quest also led him to periods of no physical affection. Priscilla longed for the old times listening to Elvis play music or holding court with friends, the times when they spent long days chatting and evenings taking the gang to all-night movie festivals or on outings to amusement parks.

Drugs remained one exploration they could make together. For years, Elvis had shared sleeping pills with Priscilla. During this esoteric phase, they had experimented briefly with street drugs. Marijuana, Priscilla says, was pleasant but made them so hungry that their weight gains convinced them to stay away. LSD was mind expanding, but one trip was enough for both of them.

All this spiritual exploration was part of Elvis' growing up. So was his decision to marry. For years he had armed himself against various girlfriends' pleas with what he called the Colonel's insistence that he stay single "for the fans." That line held Anita Wood at bay for a good five years until her exasperation overruled her understanding, and it held Priscilla —and her parents— for about the same length of time.

Just before Christmas of 1966, Elvis gave Priscilla a diamond ring: three carats surrounded by a detachable row of smaller ones. He proposed to Priscilla in her bedroom upstairs at Graceland, and the overjoyed couple ran downstairs at once, Priscilla clad in a terry bathrobe, to announce their engagement to Vernon and Dee and Elvis' grandmother. A few weeks later, the couple traveled to Los Angeles for the filming of *Easy Come, Easy Go.* They invited Priscilla's parents, then stationed at Travis Air Force Base near Sacramento, so they could tell them the big news in person.

On the eve of marriage, some men crave a last shot of wild behavior. Some drink, others have a sexual fling. Elvis embarked on a spending binge.

Two months after announcing the engagement, Elvis set his sights on a ranch near Horn Lake, Mississippi, featuring 160 acres, a little house, a barn, and a herd of purebred cattle. Simple though it sounds, the property's rolling hills suggested something different to everyone involved. To Priscilla, it suggested a cozy, newlywed getaway from the crowds of Graceland. To Elvis, it had the makings of a semicommunal, state-of-the-art ranch. He dubbed it Circle G for Graceland (which he put up as collateral to borrow the ranch's $500,000 asking price). To Vernon's practical eye, the peaceful spread cloaked potential financial ruin.

Naturally, Elvis' vision prevailed—but his father's forebodings threatened to come true. One small house wouldn't accommodate everyone, so Elvis arranged for six mobile homes to be mounted on concrete foundations. He had already transplanted horses from Graceland's stables for Marty Lacker, Alan Fortas, and the other Guys and their wives who were with him. Next, he decided, they all needed Cowboy Cadillacs. Elvis bought each of them an El Camino pickup truck. Still not satisfied, Elvis bought a truck for everyone involved with the ranch: for all the contractors installing the trailers, running water pipes, and laying additional electric lines. In a matter of weeks, Vernon was horrified to discover, his son had spent over $97,000 on pickups.

The spree continued. Plans were laid for a big, new house at the ranch for him and Priscilla. Tractors, huge horse trailers, expensive farm machinery, and power tools from Sears were bought. In the blink of an eye, the Circle G Ranch had drained the Presley reserves of one million dollars.

Elvis was manic in his enjoyment of the ranch. He wandered its acres and supervised every detail of construction. He puttered with his power tools and tinkered with the farm equipment. Recreation, equally crazed, was continual and involved everyone: Elvis, Priscilla, the Guys, their wives and kids. Everybody went skeet shooting, turtle hunting, and horseback riding, attended all-day picnics and all-night musical jam sessions. There was always a crowd.

The crowd's enthusiasm, however, went no deeper than that of Hollywood extras. The wives wanted to get back to their homes, the kids to their friends. Being short of cash, several of the Guys quietly sold their trucks. Priscilla longed for time alone with her fiancé.

An alarmed Vernon called the Colonel every day, begging him to find a project for Elvis before he spent every penny of his fortune. The Colonel quickly obliged, pulling *Clambake* from his sleeve like a magician's rabbit. Elvis kicked and groaned about having to make another awful movie, but Vernon told him he had no choice—they were going broke.

Reluctantly, Elvis hung up his ranch duds and headed back to Hollywood, where his overweight appearance shocked the Guys he'd left holding the fort in Bel Air. He'd been eating a steady country diet of corn pone, mashed potatoes, sausage gravy, and biscuits since leaving. He weighed in at a hefty 210 pounds (40 pounds over his normal weight) upon arrival, and showed every ounce.

For years, Elvis had been a yo-yo dieter, gaining weight between films, then shrinking down again for the next commitment with the aid of pills and crash dieting. Studio officials weren't aware of this pattern because Elvis struggled to stay under wraps until he could return to the limelight in his leaner state.

But this time Elvis wasn't so fortunate. He was spotted by a United Artists executive before he'd had a chance to slim down. The executive berated Elvis and served notice both to him and the Colonel that Elvis had better shape up or he'd be taken off the movie.

The wrangling over his appearance further depressed Elvis, who was already unhappy about having to leave the ranch to make another grade B flick. One night, groggy with sleep, he awoke to go to the bathroom and tripped on a television cord. A headfirst dive into the bathtub knocked him out cold. Priscilla sounded the alarm, and in no time the bedroom was swarming with friends, movie studio executives, and the Colonel.

Colonel Parker took charge, clearing out everyone but himself and the doctor, who diagnosed a concussion. The Colonel had his own thoughts on what else was ailing Elvis and seized the chance to cure the problem. He'd long blamed Larry Geller for making Elvis passive and muddle-headed and for changing him into a somber bookworm.

With his charge too weak to protest, the Colonel struck. Larry was not to be left alone with Elvis, he decreed, and would be permitted on the premises for nothing more than haircuts, supervised by himself or one of the Guys. In addition, the payroll would be cut back. Elvis couldn't afford all the cash that was leaking out every week. Furthermore, they all should quit bothering Elvis with their problems, he continued, and filter everything through Joe Esposito. Joe was now the group's foreman, and Marty Lacker would be in charge of special projects. His first task was the content of the Colonel's final pronouncement—Elvis' wedding. It was time for his boy to grow up and settle down.

The event took place just a few months later, on May 1, 1967, at the Aladdin Hotel in Las Vegas. Priscilla was 21 years old. Despite Marty's new title, the wedding was almost exclusively the Colonel's party. Nor did Priscilla or Elvis have much say in wedding details, including the guest list. For example, of the entire Memphis Mafia, the Colonel invited only Marty Lacker and Joe Esposito to witness the ceremony. Red West was so hurt and angry that he and his wife boycotted the larger reception.

The ceremony—conducted by a justice of the peace in a Las Vegas hotel—wasn't the sort of thing you'd expect from someone as spiritually committed as Elvis had always been. Nor was the wedding's timing particularly tailored to the Presleys. Within days after the ceremony, Elvis had to return to finish *Clambake*. Next, the Colonel dashed the couple's desire to tour

Europe, claiming it would annoy the fans there who had never gotten Elvis over for a concert. They grabbed a few days with Lamar Fike at the ranch, then honeymooned briefly in the rainy Bahamas.

Nine months later to the day—February 1, 1968—Lisa Marie Presley was born. Despite her mother's miniscule weight gain during pregnancy, the baby was a perfectly healthy six pounds, 15 ounces.

Renewed by happiness in his personal life, Elvis found the strength for a fresh approach to his work. He made plans to return to the concert stage after a seven-year absence and opted to do it on television—his first such appearance since 1960. He taped the NBC special *Elvis* in June 1968, and it aired to good reviews and ratings in December. Elvis was on the comeback trail.

In January 1969, that trail brought him back to Memphis for his first recording session there since his days at Sun, and certainly the most creative studio time he'd had in years. Next, he headed to Las Vegas—the only town where Elvis had ever bombed, in a two-week, 1956 engagement at the New Frontier on a shared bill with comedian Shecky Greene and the smooth string sounds of the Freddie Martin Orchestra. The middle-aged crowd did not respond warmly to Elvis, whose name slowly sank to the bottom of the marquee.

What enticed Elvis (really, Colonel Parker) to accept a Vegas booking 13 years later was the opening of a brand-new, grand hotel, the International. Touted as a colossus on the desert, the International Hotel was Nevada's tallest building with its largest body of water after Lake Mead, featuring a thousand slot machines and lavish entertainment. The Colonel figured Elvis could piggyback on the publicity the new hotel was sure to generate. An engagement at the International also would give "his boy" a chance to perfect his act before taking it on the road.

Although he started out unhappy about playing Las Vegas, Elvis soon changed his mind.

Announcing, "I don't care if I don't make any money, as long as I give a good show," he planned the show's music, choreography, costumes, and staging, assembled 50 singers and musicians—including fine studio players from Los Angeles, a pop gospel group, a soul trio, and a 35-piece orchestra plus conductor—and pulled everything together for a two-week rehearsal.

On July 26, 1969, the curtain rose on a four-week show with a one-million-dollar contract. Two thousand guests sat enthralled (when they weren't up and screaming their ovation) that night and twice every night, seven days a week, for the next month. A newly slender Elvis careened through his rock hits first, then sank with relish into more current material, such as "In the Ghetto," released in April, and "Suspicious Minds," which was getting its first airplay on its way up the *Billboard* pop chart. In early November, it became Elvis' first number one hit since 1962.

December saw the release of *Change of Habits,* Elvis' last fictional movie. The fulfillment of his contract liberated him forever from the Hollywood travelogues he despised.

Over 101,500 people had seen Elvis at the International Hotel. The response was so strong he opted to return in January 1970 instead of waiting a year as he'd planned. The January commitment rivaled the earlier show's success.

On February 24, he opened his next large-scale show on the concert trail: six performances at the Houston Astrodome. Despite terrible acoustics, the fans came in droves. Nearly 207,500 of them filled the stands during the course of the engagement, bringing him a reported $1.2 million, even though some tickets were priced as low as a dollar to allow the poorest fans to come.

In 1971, the Jaycees gave Elvis an award as one of the "Ten Outstanding Young Men of America." The plaque hangs in Graceland's trophy room. The award capped a period of great productivity and creativity. The birth of a new, mature Elvis, now a husband and father, energized him to return to his old success. This Elvis was playing a new kind of music—much lusher and more orchestrated than those earliest R&B recordings—to a far broader audience than the teenagers who first adored him.

Unfortunately, marriage and fatherhood couldn't quell all the old conflicts nor fill the loneliness that Gladys' death had wrought. These pains would prove consuming in the coming years, just as the grueling weeks on the road would take a toll on the very family life that had enabled Elvis to resume his love affair with music and live performance. The concert circuit proved a cruel mistress.

Opposite page: Striding into a Las Vegas press conference, flanked by the Colonel, at the start of a four-week gig at the International Hotel. (July 31, 1969)

Always seeming to be surrounded by fans,
even onboard an airplane, above left.

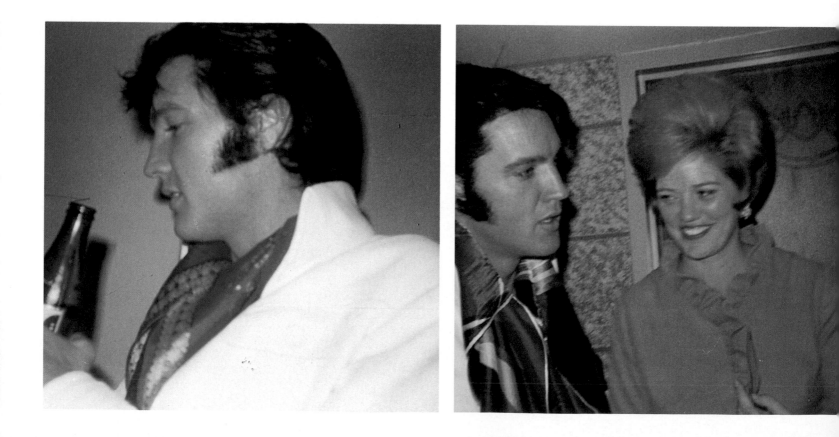

Above, Elvis with superfan Chris Trant; below, greeting fans outside his
Beverly Hills home. (1969)

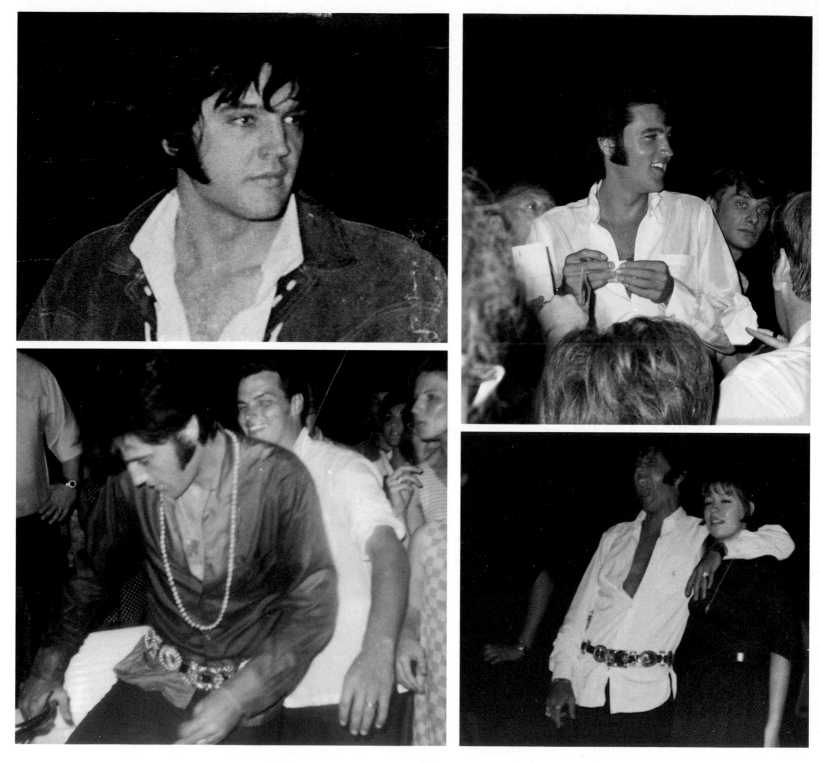

Top left, Elvis had the guards ask everyone to leave after a rare moment of annoyance with the fans. A group of fans had blocked the Graceland driveway, then shouted something nasty as Elvis drove in the front gate. Top right, learning about two girls from Mississippi Delta Junior College, who had had themselves shipped into Graceland in a crate marked as containing wolfhounds. Elvis, who didn't need any more dogs, had the crate shipped back. The girls kicked their way out; later, Elvis invited them to Graceland. Above, in tune with the times, Elvis wears love beads. Right, staying up all night with the fans. (1969)

Sunbathing in the backyard of his Palm Springs home.
Sometimes Elvis would hook up an electric fan to cool himself
while he tanned. (1969)

With fans at Graceland. (July 1970)

Opposite page: Top left, the famous musical gates of Graceland, custom built by Doors Incorporated of Memphis in 1957. All others this page, with fans who made their way backstage, Las Vegas, August 26, 1970.

Top left, around the time Elvis sold one of his California mansions to actor Telly Savalas. Top right, excited fans scream as Elvis walks back to the gate to greet them after parking his car. Above left, reaching out to give an autograph. Above right, another backstage visitor, Las Vegas, August 1970.

With superfan J. Cherry.

Around the time of Elvis' filming of *That's the Way It Is.*

Ducking so the wind won't mess up his hair, en route to the Astrodome to perform in a concert for the Houston Livestock show. (1970)

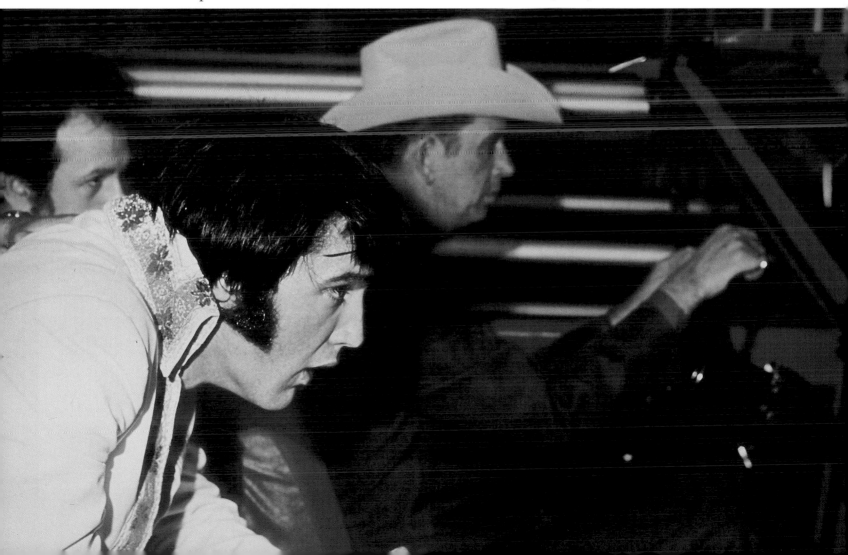

Members of the "Memphis Mafia."
From left, Sonny West, Red West,
Elvis, Jerry Shilling, Lamar Fike,
and Joe Esposito.

Standing in a jeep just before
entering the Astrodome.
Sonny West is in front.

Top and bottom left, kissing super fan Mikki Malbrough—and again with her on far left with friends in Mobile, Alabama 1970.

With fans. (1970)

With fans. Right, accepting a plaque from Norwegian fans.

Top, chatting with fans through the moon roof of his limo. Below, wearing the gold belt presented to him by the *International Hotel* after setting a Las Vegas record: 101,509 paid customers and $1.5 million grossed. The heavy belt style became an Elvis trademark. (1970)

Opposite page: Showing off to friends. Elvis had 37 weapons in his Graceland gun collection, and he enjoyed target practice with his friends. (1970)

Below left, Priscilla, George Klein, Elvis, and Barbara Little at George Klein's wedding. Elvis was best man. Below right, he and Sonny West straighten each other's carnation at Sonny's December wedding. (1970)

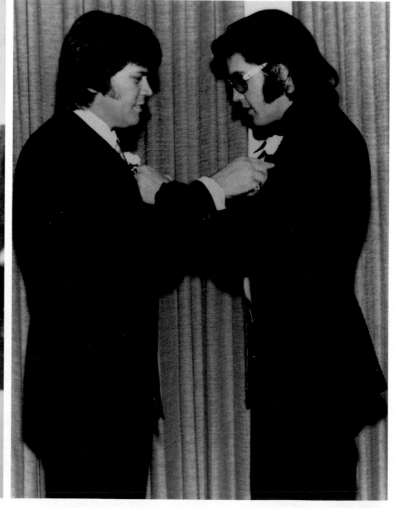

Top left and above right, showing off his gold Jaycees medallion (1972).
Above left, the theme from *2001: A Space Odyssey* was the distinctive
opening music for Elvis' concerts. (Both, November 1971)

With fans, including a Las Vegas showgirl, and left, in Seattle, April 1973 with superfan Jim Borda.

Above left, President of Elvis Presley Fan Club of Italy, Livio Monari and friend (Las Vegas, Aug. 24) on their second 1972 meeting with Elvis. When Elvis heard that their first pictures didn't come out, he invited them back. Above right, in a jeep at the Honolulu Airport before doing his *Aloha from Hawaii* satellite television special. Below, gifts for Lisa Marie.

Above left, backstage at the Las Vegas Hilton with superfans Alan and Dee Bigalow. Above right, on tour in Arizona. Below left, backstage in Las Vegas, receiving an award from superfan Virginia Coons in a meeting arranged by Tom Diskin. Below right, an Asian fan presents Elvis with a gold record. (1973)

Las Vegas, March 31, 1975—the day Elvis gave me this beautiful, white-mirrored, nail-studded jumpsuit.

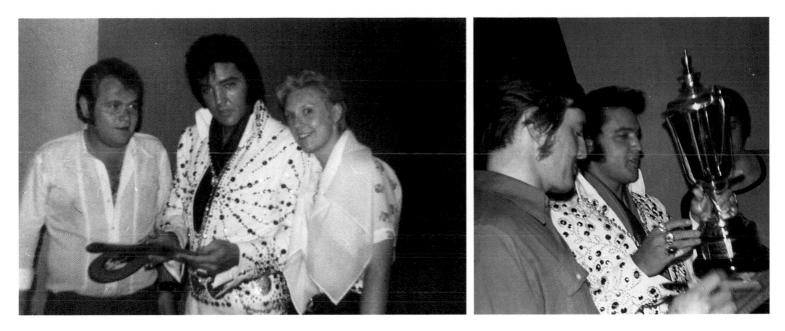

Above left, autographing a menu for International Elvis Presley Fan Club of Belgium (1973) in Las Vegas. Above right, receiving a new Musical Express award from members of Elvis' British fan club. Below, Elvis' March 3 return to the Houston Livestock Show at the Astrodome. Joe Esposito holds Elvis in by the the belt; bodyguards Red and Sonny West ride in back. (1974)

At a New York City press conference, the Colonel joked to reporters,
"Let me live up to my reputation, folks," then declared the session over.
(1972)

Opposite page: Relaxing with Lisa Marie after a hard karate workout.
(1974)

Joe Esposito helping an exhausted Elvis after a concert.

Above left, with Priscilla. Above right, acting out his lifelong fantasy of becoming a law officer in his honorary Shelby County, Tennessee, sheriff's outfit.

FINAL

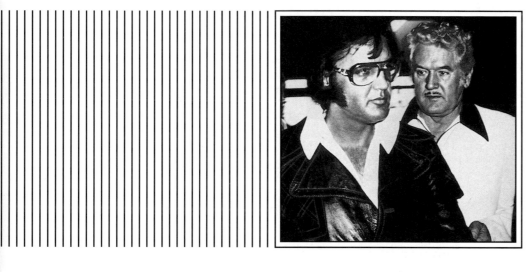

DECLINE

These photos of Elvis from the '70s tell the story of his final years. To many, he would always be the King of Rock 'n Roll. He was still beloved by millions, still a financial success. In virtually every image on these pages, Elvis is surrounded by people, whether loyal fans or members of the entourage that was one of his most prized trappings of success.

But his face has lost the innocence, the unconscious sexuality of the young man the nation first swooned over. His devilish grin is gone. The pure wonder that once played over Elvis' features has been missing for a long time. What shows in his face and physique are the years of abuse: too much stodgy food, too many drugs, too little exercise. Of all the people whose task it was to look after him, he was the most negligent. Priscilla's leaving only added to his sense of isolation.

Though her departure was a long time coming, he didn't notice the warning signs until she was heading for the door. Members of the Memphis Mafia point to what might be called Elvis' benign neglect of his young wife, with whom he gradually spent less and less time. In 1971, Elvis passed a rule: No wives or girlfriends on tour. Priscilla and the other women were allowed to come to Las Vegas only for show openings and closings, and sometimes, only for openings. Sonny West says the Presleys often didn't see each other for seven weeks at a time, and Elvis' visits home with his family were brief and restless. The time apart took its toll on the Guys' marriages, too: Jerry Schilling's, Joe Esposito's, Sonny West's.

Their boss banned the wives because he didn't want them to cramp his style. Elvis valued Priscilla's loyalty and the notion of being a family man, but he wanted freedom, too. Wild parties continued in Elvis' Palm Springs house, even after Priscilla, vacationing there with one of the wives, discovered a note in the mailbox saying

"Thanks, let's do it again soon. Lizard Tongue." Priscilla was enraged, although Elvis denied any wrongdoing and laughingly insisted the note came from an unknown fan.

The house did indeed shelter some pretty kinky scenes. Sonny West, Red West, and the other Guys would scout for attractive young women to come over and surround Elvis as he held court. The women would hope to get close to the King, and many did. Others settled for one of his Guys.

Several Guys—who had the task of finding young women to spend time with Elvis in Las Vegas and Bel Air—have said in interviews and their own writings that he couldn't bear the thought of making love to a woman who had borne a child. With Lisa Marie's birth, Elvis grew more distant, and Priscilla became irrevocably shut out. He was financially generous but sexually and emotionally withdrawn. It was many months before he could bring himself to make love to her, and Priscilla felt lonely and undesirable.

There is still some dispute over exactly when, in this period, Priscilla met Mike Stone. Oddly enough, Stone was both Hawaiian and a karate champion, echoing the character of her husband's island movies and his long-time passion for karate. He was also unhappy in his marriage and on the verge of divorce.

While several Guys had guessed at Priscilla's affair, none of them told Elvis. She could have gone on leading two lives indefinitely—such was Elvis' oblivion—but she chose to tell him. On February 23, 1972, the Presleys separated. When Elvis gathered the Guys to tell them that his wife was going off with another man, they stood in embarrassed silence. Red West, who had often heard his boss complain that Priscilla should stop bugging him and should find someone else to mess around with, broke the silence with "That's what you wanted, isn't it?" He had meant to comfort Elvis.

Elvis had one more shining hour before his terrible decline—the television special *Elvis: Aloha from Hawaii.* Planned as grand entertainment of the satellite communications era, the show was announced by Colonel Parker and NBC in the fall of 1972 at the end of Elvis' season in Las Vegas. With production costs topping two-and-a-half million dollars (including one million dollars for the star), the show from Hawaii was conceived to be broadcast live around the world, until NBC realized that in doing so it would miss prime time (and top TV profits) in many countries. Instead, the January 12, 1973 show was broadcast live to Japan, where it commanded an incredible 98 percent of the viewing audience. It was taped for broadcast two days later in Europe. An expanded version was seen in the United States on April 4.

On the show, Elvis sounded great and looked fabulous: tanned, stunningly made up and costumed, and back down to fighting weight. As Colonel Parker had long forbidden overseas concert tours, the *Aloha* special struck Elvis as a chance to finally reach out to his distant fans via satellite. He roused himself from his food and drug indulgences to meet the challenge. For three months he stuck to a rigorous diet of 500 calories per day supplemented with vitamin shots.

An estimated one billion viewers in 40 countries saw the one-hour concert, beating the audience who watched the first moon landing on July 20, 1969. The show also raised $85,000 for Hawaii's Kuiokalani Lee Cancer Fund. Known for his philanthropy, it was Elvis' choice to support this charity named for the Hawaiian composer of "I'll Remember You," which he recorded in 1966 and performed on the TV special.

Four days before the show, Elvis sued Priscilla for divorce. It was his 38th birthday. By now, Elvis was already involved with former Miss Tennessee, Linda Thompson. An outgoing, motherly woman, Linda stuck by Elvis for a good four years, until she was worn out by the despair of watching him self-destruct and the hopelessness of trying to reform him. Ginger Alden, Elvis' young fiancée at the time of his death, picked up where Linda left off in 1976.

Ginger met Elvis at Graceland with her sister, the new Miss Tennessee, and nine weeks later, on January 26, 1977, Elvis asked her to marry him. Their wedding, Ginger says, was to be on Christmas Day of that year.

Unfortunately, this brief hiatus of good health vanished, to be replaced with an astonishingly abusive lifestyle. Priscilla says, not just in jest, that cooking for Elvis was simple: She would take whatever she was fixing for everybody else and burn it. He ate a great quantity of burnt bacon, eggs, sauerkraut, and cheeseburgers, the latter usually eaten just before bed and followed by up to six banana splits. The only vegetables he ate with any regularity were fried tomatoes.

One of his favorite meals away from home was the $49.95 peanut butter and banana submarine sandwich fried in bacon grease served by the Colorado Mine Company restaurant in Glendale, Colorado; the sandwich wasn't that big, but Elvis had to fly his plane over from Memphis for a late snack of them, at a cost of about $16,000.

As the photographs in this section show, Elvis was living in the adoration of his fans, which kept him walled in at Graceland. The one form of exercise he got on a regular basis was karate. Elvis practiced this martial art for 18 years and held an eighth-degree black belt. It was he who inadvertently opened the door to Priscilla's affair with Mike Stone by urging her to get involved in the sport.

Except when locked into a Hollywood shooting schedule, Elvis maintained a life rhythm all his own that was permanently out of sync with the rest of the world's. He stayed up until the early hours of the morning, then slept as late as 4 P.M. The windows in his bedroom at Graceland, and in any of the other houses or hotels he called home while out of Memphis, were kept tightly shaded. No ray of sun contradicted Elvis' definition of morning.

But Elvis' health problems went far beyond a lack of leafy green vegetables and a normal sleep schedule. Though he rarely used street drugs, he relied on sympathetic doctors and pharmacists in many cities to stock his demand for prescription drugs like codeine, morphine, Quaalude, Valium, and Demerol. Among Elvis' daunting bedtime reading stack was always the *Physician's Desk Reference*, which he consulted to avoid overdoing his doses or making lethal combinations.

He didn't always get it right. Elvis was saved from overdoses on several occasions by his girlfriends and the Guys, and his autopsy would reveal severe heart disease, clogged arteries, and a badly distended liver.

Toward the end, Elvis worked a punishing schedule of as many as 150 concert and nightclub dates a year. Their format never varied, and he found this boredom a torture equal to that inflicted by the formulaic Hollywood travelogues in the '60s.

For many years Elvis had felt out of control of his life and destiny. Gladys' death had opened a chasm of loneliness that none of the Guys nor dozens of women were able to close. His alienation and disappointment grew over time until it overcame him. The career that the Colonel had crafted for Elvis was not the one his star had craved of musical creativity, serious acting, and overseas travel. He appreciated his fans and was always gracious to them, but their eyes constantly upon him imprisoned him behind guards and wrought iron.

In the end, all Elvis wanted was oblivion, which came on August 16, 1977. But he will never be forgotten by his millions of fans. He came and changed our lives, leaving a legacy of photographs like these, lasting music, and memories. The images on these pages show something of Elvis and how he endeared himself to us. They certainly are a poignant testament to how much we adored him. On these pages, at least—and in fans' private scrapbooks—his smile will endure, like our memories, forever.

Above left, with girlfriend Linda Thompson, whom Elvis met through George Klein on July 5, 1972. Above right, backstage in Las Vegas. Left, aboard Elvis' airplane, *Lisa Marie.* (1975)

Opposite page: Elvis first learned karate in the Army. He was faithful to its study for 18 years, ultimately reaching the rank of 8th degree black belt, or senior master of the tae kwan do arts. Bottom, meditating before a tournament.

Top left, Vernon, Dee, Linda, and Elvis at a karate demonstration. Top right, Elvis stopped his limo to help an accident victim. Left, Mr. and Mrs. Sam Thompson (Linda's brother and sister-in-law), Elvis, Lisa, and Linda. Above, with Vernon, who accompanied his son on his concert tours until 1976, when he became ill. He made one final trip with Elvis, the last TV concert for CBS.

Top, with fans—from a family to this friendly security guard. Middle right, being protected while on tour by Red West, an old school friend who served as Elvis' bodyguard for 20 years. Right, with a fan. Above, while stopped at a gas station to fill the limo, Elvis observed two men holding up the attendant—the legend holds— and shouted at them. He talked them out of the robbery, everybody shook hands, and the foiled thieves went on their way.

Top right, with pal Ed Parker, a friend who was never on the payroll, but who taught Elvis karate and guarded him on tours. Middle right, on his last snowmobiling trip in Vail, Colorado, January 1976. Above left, with Diane Goodman, Miss Georgia, whom Elvis briefly dated. Above right, with Ginger Alden at Mt. Sherman, Arkansas, for her grandmother's funeral on January 3, 1977.

Opposite page: In Hawaii on Elvis' last vacation later the same year.